LORD BEAVERBROOK
and the KENNEDYS

LORD
BEAVERBROOK
and the KENNEDYS

James Downey

The University of New Brunswick gratefully acknowledges the support of the J. William Andrews Fund in the publication of this book.

Designed and typeset by Scot Fillier with primary texts in Palatino.

Library and Archives Canada Cataloguing in Publication

Downey, James, 1939-
    Lord Beaverbrook and the Kennedys / James Downey.

Contains speeches by John Fitzgerald Kennedy and Robert
    Francis Kennedy delivered in Fredericton at the time when
    each of them received an honorary degree from the University
    of New Brunswick.
Includes bibliographical references.
ISBN 978-1-55131-164-7

    1. Beaverbrook, Lord, 1879-1964--Friends and associates.
2. Kennedy family. 3. Kennedy, John F. (John Fitzgerald),
1917-1963. 4. Kennedy, Robert F., 1925-1968. 5. Speeches,
addresses, etc., American--New Brunswick--Fredericton.
6. Canada--Foreign relations--United States. 7. United States--
Foreign relations--Canada. 8. University of New Brunswick.
I. Kennedy, John F. (John Fitzgerald), 1917-1963 II. Kennedy,
Robert F., 1925-1968 III. Title.

DA566.9.B37D69 2012   941.082092   C2011-908329-9

Publisher:
UNIVERSITY OF NEW BRUNSWICK
P.O. Box 4400   P.O. Box 5050
Fredericton, NB E3B 5A3   Saint John, NB E2L 4L5
www.unb.ca

Printed in Canada

With affection and gratitude for

Lady Violet Aitken

University of New Brunswick
Chancellor Emerita

Contents

Acknowledgements

Just as it takes a village to raise a child, so it sometimes takes a virtual village to birth a small book. Such is certainly the case with *Lord Beaverbrook and the Kennedys*.

The project began some years ago when I discovered in the archives of the University of New Brunswick the texts of two superior speeches given at that university by John Kennedy in 1957 and Robert Kennedy a decade later. I resolved that my first retirement project would be to prepare those speeches for publication, with a brief introduction to set the scene. In the event, retirement got delayed and the introduction got expanded to do at least summary justice to the complex relationships that furnish context for the speeches. In the meantime a small village of contributors has come into being and a sizeable debt has been incurred.

My first and greatest debt is to Bill Bendix who, as my research assistant, did much of the unearthing of evidence of the relationship between Lord Beaverbrook and the Kennedys. He burrowed deep into the rich archives of the University of New Brunswick and read widely in the literature of British-American relations during and after the 2nd World War.

Bill's work on this project, like my own, was supported throughout by successive archivists of the University of New Brunswick: first Mary Flagg, then Patricia Belier. Their encouragement was as important as their help, and their help was invaluable.

Many villagers have read drafts of parts of the manuscript and offered improving advice, among them Cyril Poole, Jim O'Sullivan, Tom Condon, Ann Cowan, Stuart Adam, David Johnston, John English, Ken McLaughlan, Geoffrey Downey, Bob & Bari Kerton, Doug Letson, David Trick, Mary Ellen Lepionka, Michael Gnarowski, Susan Montague, and Scot Fillier. While no doubt some infelicities of fact and expression remain, my text is much the better for my colleagues' counsel.

The design of the book is the work of my gifted artist friend Scot Fillier. It is the second book he and I have collaborated on. I hope there will be more.

Two other debts should be acknowledged. The late Colin B. Mackay, a presidential predecessor of mine at the University of New Brunswick, and a player in the story the book tells, encouraged me to undertake this project and allowed me to record an interview with him on his relations with Lord Beaverbrook during the 1950s and 60s. Mackay was president at the time of the visits of both Kennedy brothers. The late Mary Louise Lynch, Lord Beaverbrook's New Brunswick lawyer, gave me access to her correspondence with Lord Beaverbrook which is sealed in the UNB archives till 2012.

Finally, thanks are due to the University of Waterloo which supported my research in a variety of ways.

Preface

The purpose of this book is threefold: first, to make available two exceptional speeches by John and Robert Kennedy (two of only three they made in Canada); second, to describe the historical and personal contexts of the special relationship between Lord Beaverbrook and the Kennedys; and third, to illustrate the rhetorical skill and craft that informs the speeches and the American tradition of public oratory which they draw upon.

The protagonist of the story is Lord Beaverbrook. While the picture of him that emerges is sometimes less than flattering, it does lend support to the proposition that he was, in the realm of politics, the most influential Canadian of the twentieth century. This is so, in large part, because of the roles he played in the two world wars, but also because of the influence he wielded through his newspaper empire and by his relationships with leading British and American statesmen and press lords.

While there have been two comprehensive biographies of Beaverbrook, and manifold other books about him, a proper measure of his relations with American politicians, diplomats, and publishers has yet to be taken. For example, both A. J. P. Taylor *(Beaverbrook: A Biography)* and Anne Chisholm and Michael Davie *(Beaverbrook: A Life)* point out that Churchill and Roosevelt had trouble warming to each other, and thus relied on Beaverbrook to develop a friendship with the president. Beaverbrook did so, and the two became quite close. But neither Chisholm and Davie nor Taylor elaborate beyond this point. And so a complete portrait of Beaverbrook's friendship with Roosevelt has yet to be written.

The Anglo-American alliance during the war years was complex and, at times, very fragile. In the early stages of the war, when the United States was reluctant to enter, it took considerable finesse on the part of British diplomats to make sure that American support continued. Beaverbrook was instrumental here and impressed his American counterparts with his charm and confidence. He dominated conferences and discussions, even when Roosevelt and Churchill were both in the room. As Vice-President Henry Wallace once wrote, "Out of all these [British-American meetings], I have no recollection whatsoever except the dynamism of Lord Beaverbrook. He was a power house with regard to what could be done and what had to be done."

Given all this, it is no wonder Joe Kennedy should hold Beaverbrook in such esteem and value his friendship so highly. No wonder too that Joe's sons would so willingly show their own respect for their father's friend by giving two of the finest convocation addresses ever made in Canada.

I have a personal interest to declare. From 1980 to 1990 I was president of the University of New Brunswick. My chancellor during those years was Lord Beaverbrook's daughter-in-law, Lady Violet Aitken, who had succeeded her late husband, Sir Maxwell Aitken, who had himself succeeded his father. Thus the Beaverbrook family connection with UNB continued. As well it should have, for the Aitkens' benefactions to the University, the city of Fredericton, and the province of New Brunswick were and, despite recent disputes about the ownership of certain works of art, still are highly visible and valued. More than that, the legend of Beaverbrook—the local boy who became a world figure while remaining proud of his humble origins—lives on in the hearts and minds of UNB alumni. At alumni gatherings I often found myself telling stories of Beaverbrook's relations with New Brunswick, stories not told in the biographies and essays about him by mostly British writers whose focus, understandably, has been on Beaverbrook's role in United Kingdom politics and business. One of those stories grew in complexity and intrigue as I pursued it. It is the story of how John and Robert Kennedy came to visit the University of New Brunswick, and why they took care to prepare and deliver superior convocation addresses.

Images courtesy of Archives & Special Collections, Harriet Irving Library, University of New Brunswick.

Additional source: http://www.lib.unb.ca/archives/HonoraryDegrees/

LORD BEAVERBROOK and the KENNEDYS

James Downey

UNB

UNIVERSITY OF
NEW BRUNSWICK

BEAVERBROOK
and the KENNEDYS

In October 1957 Senator John Fitzgerald Kennedy (JFK) had only just been released from one of his longest and most painful stays in hospital for treatment of his chronic back injury. His wife, Jacqueline Bouvier Kennedy, was near term with their first child, Caroline. It was early in his campaign for the American presidency. In spite of these constraining circumstances he chose to spend two days visiting Fredericton, New Brunswick, Canada, where he received an honorary degree and gave the convocation address.

A decade later, in 1967, JFK's younger brother Robert Francis "Bobby" Kennedy (RFK), Senator for the State of New York, made a similar trip for the same purpose. Four years after his brother's assassination and less than a year before his own death, RFK was preparing to make his own run for the presidency.

With so many clamorous demands on their time, and with such an overarching political ambition, why would JFK and RFK not only visit a place where there was not a vote to be had but craft and deliver excellent speeches? The reason for their visiting lies in the improbable ties of friendship between their father, Joseph Kennedy, and Max Aitken, Lord Beaverbrook, Chancellor of the

John Fitzgerald Kennedy
making his UNB convocation address
October 1957

Robert Francis Kennedy
during his UNB convocation address
October 1967

University of New Brunswick. The reason for the excellent speeches lies largely in a tradition of formal oratory that thrives more in the United States than in Canada.

The friendship between Lord Beaverbrook and Joseph Kennedy came about when Kennedy was American ambassador to the Court of St. James in London during the 2nd World War. An isolationist, Kennedy believed it was folly for Britain to declare war on Germany, and he was excoriated in the British press for his views. A handwritten letter from Kennedy to Beaverbrook, in May 1938, protesting a piece in Beaverbrook's *Daily Express* brought the two together. From that point on Beaverbrook, who in the beginning shared Kennedy's pro-appeasement views, ensured favourable press coverage for the American ambassador.

As in many friendships, perhaps each man saw something of himself in the other. In this case, however, mutual attraction was very firmly buttressed by the prospect of mutual advantage. Beaverbrook did not have long to wait for Kennedy to return the favour. On May 8, 1940, as Churchill struggled to stabilize his government, Ambassador Kennedy provided Beaverbrook with critical military intelligence. American sources in Germany had discovered that Hitler was about to attack the Low Countries. When this information proved accurate, it was a boost not only for British forces but also to Beaverbrook's standing in the Churchill government. Kennedy's good turn helped cement an unlikely friendship that would withstand mutual suspicion, even betrayal, and last until Beaverbrook's death in 1964.

EMPIRE BUILDER

In one of Lord Beaverbrook's books, he quotes a political foe: "Max Aitken was born in Newcastle, New Brunswick. It was too small for him. So he went to Halifax in Nova Scotia. It was too small for him. He left for Montreal, the commercial capital of Canada. It was too small for him. He came to London. It is too small for him. He will go to hell. It won't be big enough."

Actually, Max Aitken was born in Maple, Ontario, but grew up in Newcastle, New Brunswick, the son of a Presbyterian minister. He had planned a career in law but quickly found his métier as a business wheeler-dealer. By the age of thirty he had become a millionaire, largely by engineering corporate mergers in the Canadian securities and cement industries. His vaulting ambition, and perhaps, it was said, his fear of being found out for some of his business dealings, led him to forsake Canada for England in 1910. There he formed a close friendship with the Conservative and Unionist leader (the only Canadian-born prime minister of the United Kingdom) Andrew Bonar Law. Within three months he ran for and was elected a member of parliament, and soon after, against the wishes of George V, was made a peer and chose the title Lord Beaverbrook. As Minister of Information during the 1st World War he showed his talent for propaganda, a talent he put to good use after the war when he built the *Daily Express* into the most successful newspaper in the world and in the process created a newspaper empire.

In the 2nd World War Prime Minister Winston Churchill, recognizing Beaverbrook's genius for organization, and over the objections of George VI, made him Minister of Aircraft Production, where he worked wonders in helping to equip the British air force to fight the crucial Battle of Britain. Later, to keep him in cabinet, Churchill made him Minister of Supply and, later still, Lord Privy Seal. Churchill used him also as principal go-between with President Roosevelt in an effort to gain American support for Britain's war effort.

After the war Beaverbrook continued to preside over his journalistic empire with great energy and to use his influence wherever and however he saw fit, including for the promotion of the political careers of Joe Kennedy's sons.

AN IMPROBABLE FRIENDSHIP

"The man who is consistent," wrote Lord Beaverbrook in his book *Success*, "must be out of touch with reality. There is no consistency in the course of events, in history, in the weather, or in the mental attitude of one's fellow men. The consistent man means that he intends to apply a single foot rule to all chances and changes of the universe. " Thus, Beaverbrook concluded, "Nothing is so bad as consistency."

Always fond of giving advice in his books and private letters, Beaverbrook was not always so eager to follow it himself. In the case of inconsistency, however, he seems to have practised what he preached. He worked tirelessly to defend Britain against the Nazis, for example, yet after the war frequently disparaged the British, especially for embracing socialism. He had a close personal

"The man who is consistent," wrote Lord Beaverbrook in his book Success, "must be out of touch with reality...nothing is so bad as consistency."

and professional relationship with Winston Churchill, rallying behind him during the war years and vacationing with him regularly in the post-war era, yet he sometimes ridiculed Churchill behind his back, calling him, among other things, "a terrible bore." Early in the war, when things were not going well for Churchill, Beaverbrook even tested support (and found it virtually non-existent) for his own chances of replacing him.

Churchill was not the only one to endure Beaverbrook's disloyalty. In a 1959 memoir of his friend, former Canadian Prime Minister R. B. Bennett, Beaverbrook contrived to show Bennett as both "a heroic Prime Minister who had saved Canada during the depression and yet at the same time to portray him as pompous and absurd." Harold Macmillan, who served with Beaverbrook in the Ministry of Aircraft Production, summed him up as he saw him: "He couldn't resist seducing men the way he seduced women. And once a man was seduced by him, he was finished."

Beaverbrook was indeed a curious blend of characteristics. As biographers Anne Chisholm and Michael Davie put it, he treated everyone close to him "with a mixture of charm, courtesy and ruthlessness." Certainly such a mixture characterized his treatment of his old friend Joseph Kennedy. Nevertheless, in old age Kennedy wrote letters to only two friends, and Beaverbrook was one of them. Kennedy had remained loyal to Beaverbrook, partly because he liked him, partly because there was personal advantage in the friendship, and partly because he never found out how treacherous Beaverbrook had been toward him during the war.

The exchange of favours between Beaverbrook and Kennedy makes it difficult to determine how much was strategic partnership and how much a close personal bond. The two men shared enough in common to enjoy one another's company. Self-made millionaires, they were capitalists who mistrusted the socialist tendencies of the modern state. Both were widely believed to have made their initial fortunes by shady, if not illicit, means— Kennedy in bootlegging during Prohibition, Beaverbrook through ruthless dealings in amassing shares for corporate mergers in Canada. Both had a passion for politics, the press, and films, and both were guilty of the same kinds of excesses in their personal lives. Moreover, they shared a pragmatic businessman's view of the world. Kennedy objected to wars on the grounds that they destroyed capital as well as lives, and thus he supported appeasement of Hitler. He wanted the United States to become a kind of giant Switzerland: well defended but neutral, and geared

Both [Beaverbrook and Kennedy] were widely believed to have made their initial fortunes by shady, if not illicit, means...

towards making money, not war. Beaverbrook, meanwhile, having become convinced of the German menace, brought to his work as Minister of Aircraft Production the same business acumen and demonic energy he had employed in his business operations.

Until Churchill had called him to take a major part in the war effort, Beaverbrook, like Kennedy, favoured appeasing Hitler —on the grounds that the continental powers should be allowed to destroy one another, whereupon Britain and America could pick up the pieces and restore order. He ordered his powerful newspapers,

A post WWII
Sir Winston Churchill
and Lord Beaverbrook
in southern France.

including the *Daily Express* and the *London Evening Standard*, to promote this position even after war had begun. Predictably, with these views neither man made many friends in Britain. A top advisor to Anthony Eden summarized the enmity when he noted, "Ambassador Kennedy is engaged in defeatist propaganda with Beaverbrook."

Before the war was over Kennedy had even more reason to believe that isolationism might have been the better course. He had lost a son, a son-in-law, and very nearly a second son. "For a fellow who didn't want this war to touch your country or mine," he wrote to Beaverbrook, "I have had rather a bad dose— Joe dead, Billy Hartington dead, my son Jack in the naval hospital. I have had brought home to me very personally what I saw for all the mothers and fathers of the world."

Beaverbrook fared much better both personally and politically. Though his London house was bombed, he lost no loved ones in the war, and his son Max, whose good looks and athleticism had earned him little respect from his father, turned out to be a brave and brilliant Royal Air Force pilot. In all, Max flew 161 operational missions, saw action throughout the Battle of Britain, and was credited with shooting down 16 German planes. Uncharacteristically, Beaverbrook showed the tender and solicitous

Sir Max Aitken, son of Lord Beaverbrook, Ace WWII RAF Pilot

affection and pride of a father as he "waited each night for Max's return from the skies where London was saved and he himself had been translated into another being."

Beaverbrook felt no obligation to remain consistent in his political or philosophical stance on German aggression, in part because of his son's nightly reports. In the spring of 1940, with the war going badly for Britain, Beaverbrook abandoned appeasement and worked tirelessly in Churchill's War Cabinet as Minister of Aircraft Production. In this capacity he sought America's involvement in the conflict and thus put himself at odds with his friend. Kennedy immediately detected a change between them. Beaverbrook, he wrote in his diary, "didn't talk like his old self. He talked as a minister of the Churchill Government should, I suppose, and seemed to be doing his best to sell me on the idea that things were still all right."

But things were not all right. Beaverbrook had already decided to by-pass Ambassador Kennedy and, at Churchill's urging, ingratiate himself with President Franklin D. Roosevelt (FDR) in order to foster an Anglo-American alliance and save Britain from the Nazi onslaught. To this end, he presented Roosevelt with rare gifts, including an original Kipling manuscript, and also aimed his considerable charm at the President's wife and daughter. In addition to making overtures, Beaverbrook was also mending fences. Only a few years before, he and Roosevelt had been political enemies. In 1936, Beaverbrook was among a number of London-based businessmen who helped William Randolph Hearst fund a smear campaign against Roosevelt. Hearst had already turned against Roosevelt the previous year for his promise to expand social reforms by stemming the "excessive profits" enjoyed by a handful of elites. Hearst had taken this promise as an attack aimed squarely at him.

Which perhaps it was. When Roosevelt laid out a series of tax hikes in 1935, he grinned at his Secretary of the Interior and said, "This is for Hearst." Hearst then used his vast media power to denounce the New Deal as the "Raw Deal" and to brand the President's fiscal policies as dangerous communist programs. In this way Hearst campaigned for Roosevelt's defeat in the 1936 election.

Beaverbrook's motives were opaque, but his support for Hearst was clear. William Dodd, America's ambassador to Germany, alerted Roosevelt to the scheme, and the Assistant Secretary of State, Sumner Welles, quickly confirmed Dodd's suspicions. Now, four years later, with a third-term election looming, Beaverbrook, at Churchill's behest, found himself courting and supporting Roosevelt. It is unclear if FDR ever confronted Beaverbrook about the Hearst plot, but if so their relationship did not appear to suffer as a result. In fact, Beaverbrook went from being one of the President's many enemies to becoming one of his staunchest defenders. It was in this new role that he judged it necessary to betray his friend Joe Kennedy.

CONSPIRACY AND BETRAYAL

In 1939 Hearst was teetering on bankruptcy and could not finance another major offensive against Roosevelt. Other isolationists would have to orchestrate the President's downfall. Ambassador Kennedy was only too eager to play a part. By the summer of 1940 a major rift had developed between Kennedy and Roosevelt over America's pending participation in the war. While Kennedy was determined to keep the United States out of the fighting, Roosevelt pushed slowly but persistently toward intervention. Increasingly, Roosevelt felt he could no longer rely on his ambassador. Instead he shifted diplomatic duties to a number of personal envoys, most notably Harry Hopkins, who had worked with him on New Deal antipoverty programs. Hopkins willingly promoted Anglo-American collaboration. When Kennedy learned of these manoeuvers, he was outraged and vowed revenge. At a London dinner party, he bragged to friends that he could put "twenty-five million Catholic votes behind Wendell Willkie to throw Roosevelt out."

The scheme that Kennedy and Luce hatched was simple but daring.

Beaverbrook was among those who heard the boast. Later that night, Kennedy further told Beaverbrook of a plot that he and Henry Luce had devised against the President. A long-time Republican supporter and a self-made man, Luce despised FDR. He was pleased to learn from his wife, Clare Boothe Luce, that Kennedy had a similar loathing. What Luce would not have been so happy about, had he ever found out, was that Clare likely knew of Kennedy's hostility because she was periodically sleeping with him. The scheme that Kennedy and Luce hatched was simple but daring. Kennedy would return to the United States in the last weeks of the presidential race, meet the Luces at the airport, rest briefly at the Waldorf Towers, and then go to a radio station, where, on a nationwide hook-up, he would criticize Roosevelt and endorse Willkie for president.

The two men were never able to carry out this intrigue, however, in part because Beaverbrook took critical steps to foil it. Beaverbrook knew that without Roosevelt in the White House the odds were slimmer that the Americans would continue providing arms to Britain, much less get directly involved in the war. Beaverbrook didn't hesitate: he reported all of Kennedy's activities, including the plan with Luce, to Roosevelt. Since taking his position in the aircraft ministry, Beaverbrook had surreptitiously compiled damning evidence against his friend. He gathered this evidence whenever Kennedy visited him at Cherkley, Beaverbrook's country home outside London. Kennedy would visit there frequently to relax from official duties, and sometimes to sleep with one of Beaverbrook's young researchers. Invariably, Kennedy gave the girl presents before asking her to mail some documents for him. Beaverbrook's secretary would intercept the letters, however, steam them open, copy the contents, and pass them on to her cagey employer.

Ready with his incriminating report, Beaverbrook did not contact the President in person but had William Stephenson, a fellow Canadian, code-named "Intrepid," pass the file on to Roosevelt. Stephenson was stationed in New York at the time, where he directed British intelligence. According to Stephenson, Beaverbrook had decided to "shoot down Kennedy" in the summer of 1940. He could no longer keep quiet about the ambassador's actions. "My son was shooting down Germans in the air," he explained to Stephenson later. "I was obliged to be ruthless on the ground." The breaking point came with the Luce plot, especially in light of Kennedy's growing insistence that Britain pay up front for arms received from the United States. This demand would have imperiled the Allied war effort, already stretched to the limit financially and militarily.

The report Beaverbrook handed to Stephenson outlined the Luce intrigue and listed some of Kennedy's most controversial statements, including the boast about the twenty-five million Catholic votes that he supposedly could mobilize. Years later, Stephenson recalled handing the report personally to Roosevelt: "I sat back and watched FDR across his cluttered desk. He had a way of reading, tilting the sheet from side to side. You could tell when he was angry by small signs. On this occasion the sign was the sudden acceleration in the tilting of the sheet. Then he folded the sheet very calmly, very slowly, and he tore it just as slowly and

The two men were never able to carry out this intrigue, however, in part because Beaverbrook took critical steps to foil it.

calmly into very tiny pieces which he dropped into a wastebasket. And then, in front of me, he drafted a cable to Kennedy."

CONFRONTATION

Kennedy had wanted to return to the United States in mid-October (1940), but Roosevelt made sure to delay the ambassador's flight until the end of the month. On the trip home, Kennedy received a presidential letter instructing him to refuse all questions from the press until he had cleared his answers with Roosevelt. Kennedy followed these instructions, saying little to the throng of reporters who greeted him in New York and pressured him on his rumoured defection to the Willkie camp. After forcing his way through the crowd, Kennedy called the President, and then climbed into the Jeep that Roosevelt had waiting for him.

Lyndon B. Johnson, then a young congressman, was sitting with the President when Kennedy first telephoned in New York. "Ah, Joe, old friend," Roosevelt said as he picked up the receiver, "it is so good to hear your voice. Please come to the White House tonight for a little family dinner. I'm dying to talk to you." When Roosevelt put down the phone, he looked at Johnson and drew his forefinger across his throat.

That evening the Kennedys, together with Missy LeHand (FDR's longtime secretary) and Senator James Byrnes, dined with the President. Roosevelt spent most of the evening charming Rose Kennedy, who enthused that the President had appointed her husband, an Irish Catholic, as Ambassador to Great Britain. Kennedy, meanwhile, grew increasingly frustrated by all the polite dinner conversation, wanting rather to speak privately to the President. Finally, his patience exhausted, Kennedy exploded. It was outrageous, he said, that presidential messages were sent to everyone in Britain except himself. It was equally outrageous that the State Department had treated him so "horribly" these past few years, failing to inform him of major military shipments from the United States to Britain. As he went on, Roosevelt nodded his head in false agreement.

At one point during the tirade Kennedy tried to mitigate his indignation, and perhaps salvage his dignity, by professing his constant loyalty to Roosevelt. "Mr. President," he declared, "I have never said anything privately in my life that I didn't say to you personally, and I have never said anything in a public interview

As he went on, Roosevelt nodded his head in false agreement.

that ever caused you the slightest embarrassment." It was a transparently false claim, but afterwards it gave the President a golden opportunity to ask for Kennedy's public support in the campaign. Kennedy, trapped by his own rhetoric, agreed, and Missy LeHand was asked to make arrangements for a spot on national radio. Two days later, the ambassador declared to the country: "I believe that Franklin D. Roosevelt should be re-elected president of the United States."

Roosevelt won the election that year and Kennedy resigned his diplomatic post soon after. No doubt, Roosevelt knew of Kennedy's disloyalty for a long time, but even so he seemed surprised by the revelations in the Beaverbrook report. Certainly the plot with Luce was news to the President and forced him, once and for all, to rein in his rogue ambassador. Beaverbrook had played a crucial, behind-the-scenes part in thwarting his friend and helping the President.

It would appear that Kennedy never learned of Beaverbrook's actions. There were several reasons for this. One was that Beaverbrook maintained an outward loyalty by having his newspapers continue their friendly coverage of Kennedy well after his resignation. Another reason was that Kennedy was needy for friendship. He acutely wanted to be liked, especially by the elites of England. "I have wondered sometimes," wrote his granddaughter Amanda Smith, "whether he didn't share Gladstone's sneaking fondness for a lord. He seems to have been especially susceptible to kind words from peers and royals, noting that the lords Derby or Beaverbrook ('a great admirer of mine, and a terribly smart man') had found his counsel sensible and useful." An entry in his diary for January 17, 1942, makes this point clear. He notes with satisfaction that Beaverbrook still mentioned his name often to Roosevelt, and always with "great affection." Was this a lie Beaverbrook told to keep his friend happy? If so, it was a lie Kennedy needed to believe.

After the war the tensions that had previously divided them disappeared with Allied victory, and Kennedy and Beaverbrook drew closer together. They found time to see each other frequently, often on the Riviera where they both had vacation homes. The location suggests luxurious semiretirement, quiet days in the sun, evening cocktails, exotic mistresses. Kennedy and Beaverbrook indulged themselves in sybaritic ways, but they also continued to scheme and strive. They were restless men, always looking for ways to influence the course of events, large and small.

They [Beaverbrook and Kennedy] were restless men, always looking for ways to influence events, large and small.

It soon became obvious that in Joe's remarkable sons they had vicarious means of achieving their ambitions. As Kennedy urged John and Robert into the political arena, Beaverbrook eagerly promoted them in his newspapers.

For obvious reasons, Kennedy had a far greater stake in his sons than did Beaverbrook, but he made sure that his friend got to share in his sons' successes as well as contribute to them. Beaverbrook, for his part, was a political animal and saw himself as an astute political observer. He wrote several books on British statesmen, two volumes on politicians and the 1st World War, and a personal memoir about R. B. Bennett, Canada's eleventh Prime Minister. His political views may have been suspect, but his skills as a promoter were unmatched. Kennedy knew this and thought that his sons, with their youthful appeal and charisma, would do well to enlist the master propagandist in their cause. To this end he encouraged John and Robert to visit Beaverbrook whenever they traveled to Europe.

BEAVERBROOK AND THE KENNEDY SONS

A meeting with his father's friend was always an honour for John, and he happily saw Beaverbrook on a trip to Britain in 1945. He wanted very much to impress Beaverbrook, not only because he was planning to launch his political career the following year and needed support, but also because he genuinely admired the man's many talents. During the war John had regarded Beaverbrook as a "strong" figure and even considered him "the logical successor to Churchill." Beyond this, he admired his ability to charm almost anyone he met. Beaverbrook was bold, independent, and flexible: exactly the qualities that John would go on to celebrate in *Profiles in Courage* (1956).

Robert, shyer, did not at first appear to share his brother's enthusiasm for meeting Beaverbrook, and even tried to avoid him on at least one early occasion. In 1948 Robert had just finished university and decided that a trip to Europe, followed by a tour of the Middle East, would give him a valuable first-hand experience of the world. As luck would have it, he booked passage on the same ship Beaverbrook was taking from New York to London. When father Joe learned of the coincidence, he urged his son to spend time on the voyage with Beaverbrook. Robert reluctantly agreed.

On the second night of the trip he dined with Beaverbrook, content to let the older man dominate the conversation. Beaverbrook talked in his usual manner—in short, abrupt sentences —on a range of topics. He criticized the United States and the Jews, rebuked the British, and praised Roman Catholicism as "the great hope of mankind." He talked about the war and the state of the world in general. Even though Robert said little that evening (or perhaps because he did), Beaverbrook came away from the conversation impressed. "He is a remarkable boy," Beaverbrook reported to Kennedy. "He is clever, has good character, energy, a clear understanding, and fine philosophy. You are sure to hear a great deal of him if you live long enough." Beaverbrook made these compliments, perhaps in part to please a friend, but also because he meant them. He always saw exceptional talent in Robert and treated him as his favourite of the Kennedy sons.

John and Robert had other media-magnate supporters: Joe had also recruited his friends Hearst and Luce. Hearst supported JFK in his first congressional run in 1946, while Luce backed him in his presidential effort more than a decade later. Beaverbrook, however, consistently supported John through all seventeen years of his political career. Joe always appreciated his friend's help and sent Beaverbrook regular updates on John's campaigns. He also sent Beaverbrook a letter of thanks in 1960, acknowledging, "Your papers certainly treated John

He, [Beaverbrook] always saw exceptional talent in Robert and treated him as his favourite of the Kennedy sons.

It must have delighted Beaverbrook that he was helping to shape the outcome of a U.S. presidential election.

handsomely." It must have delighted Beaverbrook that he was helping to shape the outcome of a U.S. presidential election.

If Joe Kennedy had any parental concerns, they were for youngest son Teddy and his uncertain future. Teddy seemed to lack ambition and to attract more than his share of trouble. He embarrassed the family when Harvard suspended him for cheating, and he outraged his father when he enlisted in the United States Army for a four-year stint. Relations between father and son did not improve after Teddy finished military service, for he returned to Harvard only to resume the carousing he had left behind.

Remembering (and perhaps exaggerating) his own misspent youth—gambling, drinking, and dropping out of school—Beaverbrook sent Teddy a letter of support after the cheating incident. He told him that mistakes made at eighteen did not haunt a man for long, and that many unexpected opportunities still lay ahead of him.

When Teddy married Joan Bennett in 1958, his father arranged for the newlyweds to spend their honeymoon with Beaverbrook. It was now Teddy's turn to endear himself with the family friend. Naturally the last thing the couple wanted to do was honeymoon with a man nearly eighty years of age, but they had little choice in the matter. "We almost had to go to Lord Beaverbrook's house in Nassau," Joan complained later. "Joe said to Ted and me that this good friend of mine has this lovely house in Nassau. And you should go down."

They spent four dull days at the estate, trapped in polite conversation, and only on the final evening did Beaverbrook seem to take pity on the young couple, arranging for a boat to take them to a remote island where they could enjoy twenty-four hours of much-needed privacy. This brief getaway, however, turned out to be the worst part of an already blighted honeymoon. "We were dumped there overnight," Joan remembered. "It was the worst experience of our life. It was a little cottage, practically a shack, on this tiny island, just sand. We slept on these mats. There were bugs, and it was a nightmare." This "nightmare" was actually a trick Beaverbrook played on many of his guests at Nassau, especially ones who bored him, and he was easily bored. Even in old age he thrived on pranks with a twist of cruelty.

Still, no doubt in deference to his father, Teddy sent Beaverbrook a thank-you note, making sure that the letter did not betray any of the hostility he may have felt towards the old man.

He knew that Beaverbrook had done much for the family and that he should not ignore someone so influential. His real feelings may be read into the fact that the letter was several months late. "It has been my purpose for some time," Teddy explained, "to write to you and once again express my great appreciation for your wonderfully warm hospitality which you so graciously extended to Joan and myself on our first and unforgettable visit to Nassau." It seems likely that Beaverbrook flashed his wide, wicked smile when he read these overly polite words.

In 1962, Ted kicked off his political career by going after Jack's old seat in the Senate and, as usual, Beaverbrook mustered his media resources and connections for the campaign. It was time to help lift another Kennedy son to prominence. Ted's mother, Rose, wrote to Beaverbrook about the campaign, noting that the Canadian newspapers had done much to bolster Jack's reputation and could likely do the same for Teddy now. Beaverbrook replied with the improbable claim that he could guarantee the support of Canada's English dailies and that he would work hard to convince *La Presse*, which circulated widely among Francophones in New England, to join in.

Ted won the seat easily, becoming at the age of thirty the youngest member in the United States Senate. The celebration was restrained, however, for the family urged Ted to keep a low profile, saying and doing nothing that might detract from Jack's reputation as President. The fear was that public opinion might turn against Jack—and the whole family—if a feeling of "too many Kennedys" emerged. Such feelings could flare if Teddy started drinking again. And so Beaverbrook, deeply involved in the Kennedy family plan, wrote Teddy a letter asking him to take his electoral win in stride and lie low for a while.

Joe Kennedy reciprocated Beaverbrook's friendship whenever he had the opportunity or could create one. He admired Beaverbrook's political and financial skill, but equally respected Beaverbrook the writer. He was especially fond of one of Beaverbrook's lesser-known books, *Success* (1921), a collection of short biographies about poor boys who made good—boys not unlike Beaverbrook and Kennedy—and set about finding an American publisher for an edition to which he would write an introduction. The book appeared under the title *The Three Keys to Success* (Hawthorne, 1956). The following year, as an additional honour to his friend, Kennedy established the Lord Beaverbrook Chair of Journalism at Notre Dame University. Then, in 1957, he

Ted won the seat easily, becoming at the age of thirty the youngest member in the United States Senate.

It would be the first of only two scripted speeches John ever made in Canada...

urged John to give a speech in Fredericton as a favour to Beaverbrook. It would be the first of only two scripted speeches John ever made in Canada (the second was an address to Parliament, in May 1961, on the importance of American-Canadian friendship in the Cold War era), and easily the more thoughtful and rhetorically effective.

BEAVERBROOK AS UNIVERSITY CHANCELLOR

When Beaverbrook became Chancellor of the University of New Brunswick in 1947, *The Globe and Mail* editorialized: "His appointment as chancellor is more than a recognition of his benefactions. It is a tribute to the very special qualifications that the Canadian-born peer possesses to an extraordinary degree. Contrary to what his many critics may think and say of him, he has been a great researcher after knowledge and truth—philosophically, politically and economically. In consequence, his is one of the best-stocked minds in British public life." The editorial goes on to praise Beaverbrook's "spectacular and valuable career in the service of the empire," and concludes: "Well might Canadians rank Lord Beaverbrook as their most valuable 'export'." This must have been music to Beaverbrook's ears, for he had left Canada more than thirty years before under a cloud, and some said only a step ahead of the law, for the corporate mergers that had made him a wealthy man. His reputation as a shifty businessman followed him to Britain and throughout much of his political career. After observing Beaverbrook's attempts to play both sides of the street in the early days of the 2nd World War, when he favoured a compromise peace with Hitler, H. G. Wells wrote: "If Max gets to Heaven he won't last long. He will be chucked out for trying to pull off a merger between Heaven and Hell . . . after having secured a controlling interest in key subsidiary companies in both places, of course."

His service as Minister of Aircraft Production and as close friend and advisor of Churchill during the war had rehabilitated his reputation, in Canada as well as in Britain.

The chancellor is the titular head of the university, available for ceremonial duties and to advise or assist the president when called upon. The president, in contrast, is empowered by statute to lead and manage the institution. Beaverbrook was never content to be a figurehead, however. From the start he took a proprietorial interest in the university's affairs. Some of that interest was welcomed: his commitment to furnish a proper research library, for example. His biographer, A. J. P. Taylor, said, "He at once set himself up as buyer-in-chief for the university library, though without enquiry into its most pressing needs. The library got what Beaverbrook thought good for it—Calvinist theology, [John] Knox's works, John Galt's *Annals of the Parish*, fine copies of the *Shorter Catechism* [of the Presbyterian Church]." Professor Taylor was dead wrong on one score, however: there was much consultation between Beaverbrook and the honorary university librarian, Dr. Alfred Bailey, about what books to buy. Bailey wrote, "I worked for three years and more with three assistants who did almost nothing else except prepare and process book lists, check the incoming books, and file them away for cataloguing. The books poured in, almost everything we asked for . . . In all there must have been twenty thousand or more." Beaverbrook's secretary, Margaret Ince, on whom much of the burden of coordinating the search fell, estimated that she had used 236 booksellers throughout England, Scotland and Wales, plus another 161 in London, not counting publishing houses.

There were, however, certain kinds of books Bailey was proscribed from buying: "I venture to advise you never to buy a book written about a man by his wife. There is no such thing as a good book by a wife about her husband unless you except the book about Arnold Bennett by his wife—and then only because his wife hated him." Promiscuous though he might be in his private life, Beaverbrook struck a Puritan pose when it concerned the young. Of the Kinsey *Report on Sexual Behavior in the Human Male* (1948), he advised: "You will have to consider whether you are going to put this book into the general Library or place it under control. It seems to me that, in any case, when the new Library Wing is opened, it would be better to hide it in some obscure place. And after a little time, produce it."

Intent on building a first-rate research library, Beaverbrook went beyond books and periodicals.

Intent on building a first-rate research library, Beaverbrook went beyond books and periodicals. He also provided some rare, if eclectic, manuscripts, including several purported to have been written by Louis Riel, and letters by William Pitt the Younger, Thomas Jefferson, and Lord Nelson. Inevitably, the item that generated greatest public interest was "Lord Nelson's letter to Lady Hamilton in which, as Lord Beaverbrook insisted, he accused her of infidelity."

A sample list of donors to the Beaverbrook collection, 1951 and earlier, bears eloquent witness to Beaverbrook's circle of acquaintance:

Winston Churchill, Franklin Delano Roosevelt, the Marquess of Queensbury, Lady Lloyd George, William Randolph Hearst, the Right Honourable Richard Law, the Smithsonian Institution, the Metropolitan Museum of Art, and the Carnegie Corporation.

To accommodate the larger collection, Beaverbrook decided to build a wing on the library. In his book, *A Second View of Things*, Dr. Albert Trueman, president of the University of New Brunswick from 1948 to 1953, acknowledges Beaverbrook's generosity but allows that there was one thing he could not do: "He could not provide money for, say, a building and then step aside and let the beneficiaries of his generosity get on with the job of planning." Plans for the library wing called for the use of mahogany as the finishing wood. Beaverbrook insisted instead on the use of indigenous bird's-eye maple. Nor did it stop there:

> He required me to give him a list of the books that he wanted for the open shelves of his new and lovely room. And he examined the list, item by item. I recall only two of the rejections that he made, although there were others. He absolutely refused to have the morals of young New Brunswick students corrupted by the poetic works of John Wilmot, Earl of Rochester. "No, Trueman. We won't have that in the Library!" He also deleted a book by Earl Browder, the American communist. He said he didn't object to it because it was written by a communist, but because Browder, in his opinion, was a damn fool.

The refurbished library was renamed in honour of two of Beaverbrook's closest Canadian friends, Andrew Bonar Law and R. B. Bennett.

The refurbished library was renamed in honour of two of Beaverbrook's closest Canadian friends, Andrew Bonar Law, the only Canadian to become British prime minister, and R. B. Bennett, 11th prime minister of Canada (1930-35). The Latin motto, taken from Psalm 38:21, emblazoned above the Bonar Law-Bennett Library entrance was *Ne me derelinquas, Domine* (forsake me not, O Lord). A more popular local translation, however, at least among those who feared that Beaverbrook's great generosity might one day come to an abrupt end, was "Forsake us not, your Lordship."

A more public and dramatic example of Beaverbrook's tendency to exercise unassigned authority occurred in 1953 when Dr. Trueman resigned, partly out of frustration with the chancellor. The University's governing body, following practice and policy, established a committee to nominate a successor. Beaverbrook's legal advisor in New Brunswick was Saint John lawyer, Mary Louise Lynch. In one of her letters to Beaverbrook she suggested that a certain dynamic young lawyer in her firm, Colin Mackay, would make a fine university president.

In 1953 Mary Louise Lynch, Beaverbrook's solicitor, put forward the name of Colin Mackay to succeed Dr. Trueman as UNB President.

When New Brunswick Premier Hugh John Flemming and Hugh Mackay, who were representing the province at the coronation of Queen Elizabeth II, visited Beaverbrook in London, he told the two that his preference for Trueman's successor was Colin Mackay. On returning home, the Premier informed the nominating committee of the University of New Brunswick's governing body that Lord Beaverbrook had made a choice, which prompted the members to resign in protest. The University's governing body debated what to do. Colin Mackay used to tell the story of a lengthy meeting of the senate from which his uncle Hugh wearily returned to tell him, "Well, it's unanimous. None of them want you." When word of all this reached Beaverbrook, he promptly resigned as chancellor. As Dr. Bailey described it:

> The provincial government pleaded with him to reconsider. . . Before long the government decided to introduce a bill in the legislature to reappoint him under the slightly different title of "Honorary Life Chancellor." They asked the new President, Colin B. Mackay, to draft the substance of the act with this end in view, and he asked me to work on it with him. Knowing how much Beaverbrook regretted having been born in Maple, Ontario, rather than New Brunswick, I made the suggestion that he be referred to in the Act as "a native son of New Brunswick," and this was accepted by the government.

Thus Beaverbrook was appeased. In a letter that fall to Mary Louise Lynch, he offered some advice to the new president: "I hope the boy Mackay will stand up to his responsibilities. He should guard against quick answers and repartee is out of the question." Beaverbrook also commented on his own part in the choice: "You mentioned Colin Mackay to me. I mentioned him to Premier Fleming [sic] and Hugh [Mackay}. The name met favour with both of them. Now he is said to be my boy. I will have to get acquainted with him."

Nevertheless, before it had all been transacted, Beaverbrook managed to find a suitably clever way to show his displeasure at how UNB had treated him. At the same hour that Mackay, the youngest university president in Canada, was presiding at his first convocation in Fredericton, Beaverbrook was receiving an honorary degree from St. Thomas University less than one hundred

Youngest Canadian University President of the day, Colin Mackay, orchestrated a quantum expansion of UNB into 22 new campus buildings during his 16-year presidency...together they [Mackay and Beaverbrook] were a formidable team.

miles away, in Chatham, thereby stoking apprehension that he was about to shift the focus of his largesse.

Summing up all this, A. J. P. Taylor said, "[Beaverbrook] imagined that he could appoint a university president, just as he appointed a newspaper editor, and the event showed that he could. Mackay proved to be an energetic president, devoted to Beaverbrook's interests." Taylor got it half right. The other half seems to be that Beaverbrook was equally devoted to Mackay's interests, at least to the extent that those interests bore on strengthening and expanding UNB. Where Trueman, by his own admission, had chafed at the peremptory style of the chancellor, Mackay knew a mentor when he saw one. It helped that he was young and anxious to learn. It helped that he was Beaverbrook's choice, and the choice widely known. It helped even more that Mackay was a quick study and determined to make a success of the job to which he had so controversially been appointed. The celebrated Oxford historian, Professor A. L. Rowse, who visited UNB in the early 1960s at Beaverbrook's behest to receive an honorary degree, witnessed Mackay at full stretch and described him as "a lean greyhound of a young man" hungry for power— one who would make a good Prime Minister of Canada.

But if Mackay nourished ambition of that sort he was too smart to let it interfere with his work as president. He was savvy enough to know where his leadership initiatives would be effective and where they would likely be resented. He was quite content to let professors Alfred G. Bailey (a distinguished humanist) and Frank Toole (a distinguished scientist) manage UNB's academic affairs, while he concentrated on getting the resources needed for a quantum expansion that included 22 new buildings during his sixteen-year presidency. And in getting resources the chancellor was invaluable. While during those years Beaverbrook did not himself build any major facilities at UNB, he was crucial in persuading government and wealthy friends to contribute to the university's fundraising campaigns.

The partnership, however, was at times hard on Mackay. On the day of the public sod-turning for the first women's residence on campus, Beaverbrook instructed him to name it after Lady Dunn, wealthy widow of Beaverbrook's good friend, Sir James Dunn, even though the president had promised the Associated Alumnae that the residence would be named after UNB's first woman graduate, Mary Kingsley Tibbits. Mackay knew people would be upset, but the prospect of attracting some of Lady Dunn's fortune to UNB was simply too alluring to sacrifice to sentiment. The gambit failed, however. Lady Dunn, who married Lord Beaverbrook a year before his death in 1964, would never make the contribution hoped for, even after she became Lady Beaverbrook.

Mackay would, by his own reckoning, lose 8 to 10 pounds during Beaverbrook's annual fall visits to New Brunswick, such were the demands "the old man" made of those around him. Yet Mackay was generous in his assessment of Beaverbrook's motives and actions. "UNB could not have grown as fast as it did without Beaverbrook," he once said. It is equally true that UNB could not have grown as fast or as strong without Mackay. Together they were a formidable team.

BEAVERBROOK'S PHILANTROPY

Not all of Beaverbrook's New Brunswick interests and benefactions were academic or cultural in nature. In all of them, however, the *modus operandi* of his philanthropy was the same, regardless of the gift. Witness "Cherkley Beneficent," the champion Ayrshire bull he gave to the province. Between June 1947 and July 1948 there was a steady drizzle of correspondence among the Maritime Stock Breeders Association, the Canadian Ayrshire Breeders Association, the New Brunswick Minister of Agriculture, A. C. Taylor, and Beaverbrook. Taylor confirms Beaverbrook's preference that the bull not be used 'artificially,' but rather that he should "enjoy his labours." After a full discussion in cabinet, Taylor accepted the bull on behalf of the province, but not before reassuring Beaverbrook that the donor would receive regular reports on the bull's activities and condition.

There have been some who felt that Beaverbrook's benefactions were little more than self-aggrandizement. Malcolm

Muggeridge visited Fredericton in the fall of 1963 to write an article for *Maclean's Magazine* on Lord Beaverbrook. What he saw did not please him. "Lord Beaverbrook has conferred many benefits on New Brunswick," Muggeridge acknowledged, "but not by stealth; his right hand has not only known what his left hand was up to, but has eagerly cooperated. It may be said, without exaggeration, that his name is as prevalent there as in the columns of his newspapers, and that its mention is as liable to produce among Frederictonians the same faint twinge, the same perceptible lowering of the voice, as among his journalistic employees. In New Brunswick Lord Beaverbrook is his own personality cult."

"In New Brunswick Lord Beaverbrook is his own personality cult."

–Malcolm Muggeridge

Those who worked closely with Beaverbrook thought differently. Presidents Trueman and Mackay, and Dr. Bailey, though frequently inconvenienced, sometimes browbeaten, and occasionally hurt by Beaverbrook's caprice, all shared the view that he was crucial to the development of their university. And what he got for UNB was as important and impressive as what he gave. He used his connections in the business world to solicit large sums of money for UNB's ambitious building program in the '50s and '60s, and his considerable influence with New Brunswick governments to get them to provide the operating funds for the rapid expansion that took place during that period. He also used his fame to bring UNB to the attention of world leaders in politics, business, the arts, and the academy.

But what was in it for him? He was a world figure who had been a multimillionaire (or a "Maxi-millionaire," as he was fond of saying) before he was thirty, knighted at thirty-two, and made a British peer at thirty-eight. He had played essential, acclaimed roles in both world wars, was on a first-name basis with most of the leading figures of the age, and had become one of the greatest press barons of all time. What attracted him to spending a significant part of each year in Fredericton and taking a keen interest in its institutions and affairs?

He, [Beaverbrook] was a world figure who had been a multi-millionaire (or a "Maxi-millionaire," as he was fond of saying) before he was thirty, knighted at thirty-two, and made a British peer at thirty-eight.

The rewards were intangible but real. According to Colin Mackay, Beaverbrook had felt that there were gaps in his early education and knowledge, especially in the fields of literature and the arts. Through the University of New Brunswick, the Beaverbrook Art Gallery, and the Beaverbrook Playhouse, he believed he could provide young New Brunswickers with the experiences and opportunities he had missed as a youth but discovered so abundantly in later life. His return to Fredericton each year was an opportunity to witness, test, and be thanked for the benefits of his beneficence. For a man often reviled by the British elite, and who could never have been elected chancellor of an Oxbridge college, New Brunswick's adulation must have been very satisfying.

Socialist leader and Beaverbrook-admirer Michael Foot said, "He was a rampaging individualist . . . and he always favoured the rambustious, marauding private enterprise system." Beaverbrook's chancellorship gave him another bully pulpit for those views, which he used in his first address as chancellor in 1947 to the graduating class at UNB, invoking the examples of John Calvin ("my master") and Winston Churchill to bolster his argument that individualism, not collectivism, is the load-bearing beam of a society's or nation's success. It was improvisation, not planning, which had won the War, and it will be improvisation that will win the peace. "But in peace, as in war, do not tread too long the way which paralyzes individualism or the power to act will be atrophied. Minds will be hedged about with fears and indecisions. The art of dealing with the unexpected is lost when a man is waiting on a machine, an organization, or a committee. And the lamps of passion and conviction burn low when we do not seek by every instrument of persuasion or education to maintain the individual's judgment and conscience. There is no substitute for the individual."

In a speech he gave three years later at Bishop's University, he reiterated this theme:

> I give you my own beliefs. A university exists to maintain standards and should seek always to raise them. It must declare war on the shoddy and the second-class. It must aim at the highest and demand the best. The temptation to do otherwise is strong today. The tendency to make the path easier—which is both natural and praiseworthy—can easily degenerate into a toleration of things that fall before the top level. Democracy itself can be distorted into a

For Beaverbrook, individualism, not collectivism, is the load-bearing beam of a society's or nation's success.

creed of equality. But if universities do not insist upon inequalities of talent and achievement, how can they urge and exhort young people towards greater exertions and finer achievements?

Then again, the modern cult of the state emphasizes the public duty of conforming to the regulations of authority. By doing so, it limits, discourages and frowns upon all demonstrations of individuality.

Anybody can see that, if this process were to succeed, the result would be disastrous. But the state seems to be incapable of halting the headlong course which it is following.

It has always been part of universities to maintain the value of the individual, to exalt him and glorify him at the expense of all institutions which threaten him.

Now this task becomes an urgent duty.

These two functions of the university must never be lost sight of. In my opinion, they excel in importance even the task of providing educated and competent young people to fill posts of responsibility in industry and the professions.

This speech by Beaverbrook stands in stark contrast with the UNB speeches of JFK and RFK. Whereas Beaverbrook stresses the primacy of the individual, the Kennedys emphasize the importance of society and collectivist action, of being each other's keeper. Not surprising then that each brother, while expressing admiration for Beaverbrook, is careful not to be construed as holding his views. As JFK put it, "Lord Beaverbrook's views and editorial declarations may often be at odds with our own individual attitudes, but one is grateful for the candor, and clear formulation of his opinions, which often act as powerful antidotes and stimulants even when they do not entirely persuade."

JFK COMES TO UNB

The University of New Brunswick lays claim to being the oldest English university in Canada, having been founded as the Academy of Liberal Arts and Sciences in 1785 by American loyalists fleeing the revolution. For most of its first century it was a classical-education college for the sons of gentlemen. In the early 1860s, however, it was transformed into a land-grant style institution, offering the first engineering courses in Canada. It admitted women in the 1880s but grew slowly through the first half of the twentieth century, in keeping with the economic development of the province. By 1947, when Lord Beaverbrook became chancellor, UNB had a student population of just over 1200. Change and growth were needed and, in post-war Canada, possible. Together with Colin B. Mackay, the dynamic young president he had chosen, Beaverbrook led the transformation of UNB over the next decade into a comprehensive university, responsive to the higher-educational and research needs of its province.

This transformation was made possible in part through his philanthropy. He provided scholarships, built the library's collections, and persuaded his wealthy friends to be similarly generous. In addition, to boost the university's reputation, Beaverbrook invited men and women of international renown (most of whom he knew personally) to receive honorary degrees, hold seminars, and give convocation speeches. Honorees included Linus Pauling, Krishna Menon, Margaret Chase Smith, A. L. Rowse, and Brendan Bracken. A few others, including Salvador Dali and Nikita Khrushchev, reluctantly declined.

Even in this context John F. Kennedy's arrival in Fredericton to receive an honorary degree was a singular event, at least for those who followed world affairs. The Kennedys had been featured in America's most popular magazines all through the 1950s, and by 1957 it was clear that John had his sights set on the presidency. Even Beaverbrook, who had consorted with the world's most powerful men, beamed at the prospect of JFK's visit.

L to R: UNB President Colin MacKay, John F. Kennedy, Lord Beaverbrook

The day before, he wrote to a friend that Fredericton "is lively again with the arrival of Senator Kennedy and the multitude that has come to see him." At a gala dinner the night before convocation, attended by many Atlantic provinces dignitaries, including the three premiers, Lord Beaverbrook, in his introductory remarks, had confidently predicted JFK's ascendancy: "When he has become the president of the United States of America, I say to him, remember New Brunswick. Full development of the Beechwood Power Project on the St. John River depends largely on water storage in the State of Maine. Remember us in the days when you are become President and give us a great dam in the State of Maine."

Lord Beaverbrook: "When he has become the president of the United States of America, I say to him, remember New Brunswick."

The city was lucky to host Senator Kennedy, not only because wherever he went he received more attention than most Hollywood celebrities, but also because he was handicapped by painful health problems at the time. After twenty-two post-operative days, doctors had released him from hospital on October 1, 1957, just a week before his appearance in Fredericton. Injuries sustained during his *PT 109* days had caused recurring back pain, sometimes so severe that he could not lift himself out of bed. In the previous two years, he had been hospitalized nine

At dinner on the evening prior to his convocation address John F. Kennedy, standing; seated L to R, Lord Beaverbrook, Hon. A.J. Brooks, and NS Premier, Robert Stanfield.

His address...
a rhetorical 'tour
de force' blending
reason, wit,
humour,
metaphor,
apt illustration,
authoritative
reference,
and a perfect
peroration story.

times. The most recent stays, which were also some of the longest, forced him to cancel many speaking engagements or have his brother Robert, among others, appear on his behalf. That he made it to New Brunswick for the October 8 convocation was little short of miraculous, and Beaverbrook would have known that his friend Joe Kennedy had prevailed upon his son to come.

For his convocation speech the charismatic young senator could easily have made do with a few conventional remarks. His mere presence was enough for gown and town alike. His address, however, was as politically astute and directed as if he were already a presidential candidate and counting on listeners' votes. It was also a rhetorical *tour de force* blending reason, wit, humour, metaphor, apt illustration, authoritative reference, and a perfect peroration story.

In presenting Kennedy, the University Orator, Robert E. D. Cattley, in the tradition of academic address, paid florid tribute to the honouree.

The Kennedys of Massachusetts are a handsome, restless, close-knit and irresistible clan, whose vocabulary has never been burdened with the word "rust".

The protagonist of the present generation stands before you. Jack Kennedy, who could have had leisure with literary fame, accepted as a virtual legacy and in the spirit of the knight-errant the challenge of a political career. With visor down, he has never allowed wealth to relax or pain to paralyze his fibers; marriage to soften or sorrow to blunt the hard steel of his purpose.

In him, as you will shortly experience, are charm tempered by caution, eloquence informed by research, and an independence of judgment warped by no partisan loyalties. Armed with this invincible combination, he won his seat as a Democratic member for Congress at the age of twenty-nine. At thirty-five he stormed his way into the United States Senate, to represent a Massachusetts that was heavily pro-Eisenhower. It took four and a half years of planning and stumping to do it—a campaign that exhausted his lieutenants as thoroughly as it defeated his deeply entrenched opponent. Last year he missed by a handful of votes the Democratic nomination for Vice-President.

In the eyes of political friends and foes he is destined for the highest office in the Union. Small wonder, seeing that he has proved many times his dedication not to one but all its forty-eight states.

May health, strength and the Kennedy star attend him, his country, and through his country our anxious world, which can use one of his breed and talents; they limn the profile of a man who has courage, not to 'love Caesar less but to love Rome more'.

For once a convocation speech lived up to the promise of its billing. Kennedy was serious in his presidential ambitions, and even a speech made in a remote town, in a taken-for-granted country, demanded eloquence, wisdom, insight, and originality.

Kennedy's "Good Fences Make Good Neighbours" speech, likely co-authored by Theodore Sorensen, centred on Canadian-American relations. But while the speech received press coverage across Canada, only in New Brunswick was it a front page story. When JFK won the presidency in 1960, however, his UNB speech suddenly became the topic of much discussion among journalists, politicians, and policymakers. As one Ottawa columnist noted,

"It is treated, nowadays, with all the respect which is accorded automatically to an important and…above all…to a significant document. Washington correspondents of Canadian newspapers wouldn't be caught without it. The various departments of the Canadian Government have examined it, scrutinized it and dissected it. Experts in Canadian-American relations have gone over it with a fine-tooth comb in search of passages which might be expected to have special meaning for our time."

The scrutiny was largely irrelevant, however. The Kennedy-Diefenbaker years would be filled with animus and mistrust between the two leaders. "He's a hothead. He's a fool —too young, too brash, too inexperienced, and a boastful son of a

When JFK won the US Presidency in 1960 Canada's oldest official student publication, The Brunswickan, celebrated with this cartoon and a reminder of its prediction three years earlier.

bitch!" is how the fervent Canadian-nationalist Prime Minister described the American President to Canadian broadcast journalist Knowlton Nash in 1962. Meanwhile Kennedy told friends that Diefenbaker was a "grandstanding, insincere, sanctimonious, platitudinous old bore." Robert Kennedy would say, years later, "My brother really hated John Diefenbaker. He thought him a contemptible old fool. In fact, you know, my brother really hated only two men in all his presidency. One was Sukarno and the other was Diefenbaker."

There were policy differences between Canada and America, of course, as always, but it was the visceral antipathy between Diefenbaker and JFK that led Knowlton Nash to conclude, "[The] repercussions of their animosity spread across the whole canvas of politics, officialdom, and bureaucracy. In some cases, normal Canada-U.S. relations simply collapsed." When Diefenbaker's Conservative government was defeated by Lester Pearson's Liberals in the spring of 1963, Diefenbaker blamed his defeat on Washington, describing it as a Kennedy-engineered *coup d'état.*

In October of 1957, however, all of this was in the future. Kennedy could not have anticipated the mutual antipathy when he gave his UNB speech and made reference to the new Diefenbaker government. In retrospect, it is clear how his strong continentalist theme might be interpreted as a challenge to the nationalist Prime Minister. Diefenbaker saw it as his God-given mandate to protect his nation's sovereignty against the rapacious Americans, just as his hero, Sir John A. Macdonald, had done at the birth of Canada.

The title of JFK's speech was a line from the Robert Frost poem "Mending Wall." Kennedy had an appreciation for poetry. He especially valued Frost, whose presence at his inauguration heralded a different kind of president. In a ceremony at Amherst College less than a month before his voice was silenced forever, JFK paid tribute to Frost and all of America's writers and artists in a finely crafted speech: "The great artist is thus a solitary figure. He has, as Frost said, a lover's quarrel with the world. In pursuing his perceptions of reality, he must often sail against the currents of his time. This is not a popular role. If Robert Frost was much honored in his lifetime, it was because a good many preferred to ignore his darker truths."

One of Frost's "darker truths" that JFK embraced was "good fences make good neighbors." It was, in retrospect, natural to choose this Frost line as the subject of a convocation address on Canadian-

Knowlton Nash:
"...repercussions of their animosity [Diefenbaker / JFK] spread across the whole canvas of politics, officialdom, and bureaucracy. In some cases... relations simply collapsed."

American relations. The new government in Ottawa had just announced it would be seeking greater economic and political independence from the United States by fostering a stronger trade alliance with Great Britain. Presidential-aspirant Kennedy used this occasion to answer Diefenbaker, not by rebutting or rebuking him, but by reminding his Canadian audience of what he considered a greater, continental destiny.

The first five paragraphs of the speech engage the audience and establish context. In a few deft sentences, JFK ingratiates himself with his listeners by showing that he knows who they are and where he is, and by paying tribute to their city, their university, and their favourite famous native son. But he is careful not to overdo it: flattery is fine, fawning is not. With a subtle blend of humour and candour he avoids appearing glib.

The romancing continues: the speaker is aware of ties between New Brunswick and Massachusetts, "ties of history, ties of kinship and ties of inseparable destiny"—"inseparable" working the more effectively for being the only modifier in the phrase. There follows a sympathetic allusion to those who, during the War of Independence, remained faithful to the British Crown and sought a new life in Canada for themselves and their descendants, some of whom were in the audience. In this context there is a pleasing irony in the reference to Charles Wentworth Upham, an early New Brunswicker who returned to the U.S. and became an uncle by marriage of one of America's most famous Supreme Court justices, Oliver Wendell Holmes.

The stage has now been set. JFK has demonstrated his empathy and his authority. The audience is his to lead, and he wishes to take them toward a serious destination: a clearer understanding of the political and economic issues that currently threaten to divide Americans and Canadians. He acknowledges that the new Canadian government has a mandate to explore closer trade connections with Great Britain, but he trusts that this is not an either/or choice: "Canada has achieved a national strength and prestige which simply does not allow any portrayal of the country as an appendage of either Great Britain or the United States."

Having tapped into a vein of patriotic pride, JFK moves skillfully to his central and somewhat controversial thesis: more than ever, the U.S. and Canada must be continental partners, with natural resources to husband, with coastlines to guard, with a common heritage to cherish. It is true that "the very closeness of our interests and national aspirations have recently brought new frictions and irritations to the surface"—disputes over the use of the water of the Columbia, Yukon, and St. John rivers; toll levels on the St. Lawrence Seaway; fishing rights; disposal of agricultural surpluses; the extent of American investment in Canadian enterprises; and the fear that Canadian culture will be drowned out by "a loud cacophony south of the border." But Canada, he says, should not revert to old habits of economic protectionism. Instead it should display a self-confidence commensurate with its importance, and embrace a robust continental partnership with the United States. Such an arrangement would not produce the hegemony of American culture, as so many Canadians fear, but rather will ensure a bright, prosperous future for both countries.

Thus JFK assures his audience that he knows the issues and is aware of Canadian public opinion about them. Part of the answer, he says, lies not in drawing apart but in improving "the machinery of joint consultation and management." The other part resides in the ability and willingness of national leaders to understand the crucial issues and avoid an outbreak of mutual economic retaliation. "If the Canadian government is in fact able, as intimated at the recent Commonwealth Conferences at London and Mt. Tremblant, to divert a larger portion of its trade to Britain, this should not be occasion for the United States to launch a new program of economic retaliation and harassment."

This seems a generous gesture, but it sets a rhetorical trap, for the injunction cuts both ways. "Likewise, I feel that the Canadian Government would gain little by approaching the matter of American business influence in too narrow a context. . . . It would be a pity to rigidify the Canadian economy merely for the sake of breaking lances with phantom American colonialism." Who can argue when put like that?

he wishes to take them toward ...a clearer understanding of the political and economic issues that threaten to divide Americans and Canadians.

His political point made, JFK shifts the grounds of his reasoning from the logical to the ethical, and in so doing taps into a vein of sentiment entirely appropriate to an academic convocation. "Today, if the United States and Canada, with their common language, common history, common economic and political interests and other close ties cannot live peacefully with one another, then what hope is there for the rest of the world?" Now it only remains to bring this lofty statecraft speech to a soft landing in the minds and hearts of the graduates seated before the speaker.

Affirming the value of education, singling out the host institution as a shining example of excellence, and celebrating the potential of the young to meet the world's problems are staple themes of convocation addresses. But if the speaker is to hold his listeners' minds and hearts to the end, he must blend gravity with levity. His audience learns what the whole world would soon discover: that JFK was expert in blending wit with serious discourse. A joke at the expense of politicians, plus a humorous

His audience learns what the whole world would soon discover: that JFK was expert in blending wit with serious discourse

story about Jonathan Swift at Oxford are mobilized to prepare the audience for the peroration.

The conclusion to a convocation speech, like the conclusion of a good sermon, should cause listeners to vibrate with a warm and quiet rapture. A poignant story always helps, especially an historical one that tells of human character and leadership. The account of Colonel Davenport and the Connecticut House of Representatives is perfect for the purpose.

> In his book, "One Man's America," Alistair Cooke tells the story which well illustrates this point. On the 19th of May, 1780, as he describes it, in Hartford, Connecticut, the skies at noon turned from blue to gray and by mid-afternoon had blackened over so densely that, in the religious age, men fell on their knees and begged a final blessing before the end came. The Connecticut House of Representatives was in session. And as some men fell down in the darkened chamber and others clamoured for an immediate adjournment, the Speaker of the House, one Colonel Davenport, came to his feet. And he silenced the din with these words: "The Day of Judgment is either approaching —or it is not. If it is not, there is no cause for adjournment. If it is, I choose to be found doing my duty. I wish therefore that candles may be brought."

It is a perfect ending to a masterful speech, a speech with serious and topical content, leavened with learned wit, and blending Aristotelian proofs of logic, ethics, and pathos in just proportions. In a thirty-minute talk, JFK had sought to allay Canadian apprehensions of American imperialism, challenged the Diefenbaker nationalist agenda, and left his audience humming with pride and hope.

"MAY JOE FIND SOLACE"

Just before JFK assumed the presidency, Beaverbrook sent a letter of congratulations to Joseph Kennedy: "Looking back now on your own career, I am convinced that had you not had to strive so hard in your early years for money...you would have had a term or two in the White House yourself." Whether sincere or not, Beaverbrook, in making this flattering conjecture, touched on the only tinge of regret that the father could possibly have felt in 1960. With John as President and Robert as Attorney-General, it likely mattered little that Joe's personal ambitions had gone unfulfilled: the universe was unfolding as it ought.

In November of 1963, that universe collapsed. When President Kennedy was assassinated, Beaverbrook sent his friend another communication, one that now seems somewhat unfeeling. "May Joe find solace," Beaverbrook wrote to Rose, "in the assurance that Robert will repeat John's career." This was not the sort of condolence one would expect. The world was shocked, the family was grieving, but Beaverbrook, it seemed, was looking forward to a new round of Kennedy achievements. As insensitive as the letter appears, it should be observed that Beaverbrook's pragmatic view of the death was consonant with what had happened once before in the Kennedy family, when Joe had coped with the death of Joe Junior by transferring all his hopes and expectations to John. It now seemed by the same logic that it was Robert's turn. Beaverbrook had participated in the family plan for nearly two decades and he was probably right to assume that Joe would find comfort in his note.

Beaverbrook had participated in the [Kennedy] family plan for nearly two decades and he was probably right to assume that Joe would find comfort in his note.

Another reason for Beaverbrook's seeming lack of a sense of personal loss may have been that he did not value highly JFK's political record and believed that the United States would be better off without him. As he explained to a Canadian friend, "The effect of Kennedy's death is, of course, bad—but not so bad as many newspapers report." Beaverbrook felt that John had mishandled the Cuban missile crisis and hoped that, with Lyndon Johnson at the helm, the United States would move toward detente with the USSR.

The people of Fredericton did not share Beaverbrook's seeming indifference to the tragic loss of President Kennedy and proposed a memorial plaque in his honour, still proud that he had visited their city six years before. Officials decided to place the plaque in a downtown square, close to a large bronze statue of Beaverbrook wearing his chancellor's robe. Beaverbrook made no public objection to the site, but said privately that he would donate money towards the plaque only if it were placed somewhere else. He was too old and feeble, however, to make a fuss, and he died before the unveiling of the memorial in 1965.

FATHERS AND SONS

A significant difference between Lord Beaverbrook and Joe Kennedy was their performance as fathers. Kennedy was remarkably devoted, supportive, and attentive. He imbued his sons with his own competitive spirit, and never failed to be engaged with their lives and careers. He set up income trusts for his children so that they might choose careers of public service if they so wished. Ralph Martin, whose *Seeds of Destruction* is the most thorough analysis of relations between Joe Kennedy and his sons, summed up the difference Joe made: "Had Joe Sr. left them alone to live their normal lives, Joe Jr. might have become a commercial pilot; Jack, an English teacher; Bobby, a social worker; and Teddy, perhaps, a playboy. Instead, their father directed their lives, almost step by step, with a combination of arrogance and loyalty and love." In summing up what his father represented to the family, Robert Kennedy confirmed the last part of this assessment:

> What it really adds up to is love . . . the kind of love that is affection and respect, order, encouragement, and support. Our awareness of this was an incalculable source of strength, and because real love is something unselfish and involves sacrifice and giving, we could not help but profit from it.
>
> Beneath it all, he has tried to engender a social conscience. There were wrongs that needed attention. There were people who were poor and who needed help. And we have a responsibility to them and to this country. Through no virtues and accomplishments of our own, we have been fortunate enough to be born in the United States under the most comfortable conditions. We therefore have a responsibility to others who are less well off.

Such a tribute could not be paid to Beaverbrook, who never performed so poorly in any of the manifold roles he played as in that of father. Perhaps he lacked the capacity for self-subordination necessary for taking a greater interest in someone else's happiness than his own. Perhaps he lacked the patience necessary for effective parenthood; he was easily bored, with adults as well as children, and often said so in their presence. Perhaps he was incapable of hiding his disappointment that none of his three children was as brilliant and fixed upon success as he had been, that none had inherited his devotion to the potent amalgam of business, politics and journalism. Whatever the cause, the effect was a generally distant, capricious, and sometimes callous father, capable of berating and humiliating his children in the presence of friends—his own and theirs—and incapable of the shows of

Here Beaverbrook is seated on the embankment of the St. John River close to where his renowned Beaverbrook Art Gallery would be built.

Lord Beaverbrook and the Kennedys

affection, respect, encouragement, and high expectations at which his friend Joe Kennedy excelled.

As time passed and his own passionate engagements with politics, journalism, business, and mistresses abated, Beaverbrook became a more indulgent and supportive grandfather than he ever was a father. He took particular interest in his oldest grandchild, Jean Campbell, who showed some of the journalistic talent he possessed. But, ironically, it was from the formidably talented writers whom he gathered round him that Beaverbrook evoked the strongest feelings of paternal affection. Journalist and politician Michael Foot, for one: "I loved him, not merely as a friend but as a second father, even though throughout I had . . . the most excellent of fathers of my own." Historian and biographer A. J. P. Taylor, for another: "I loved Max Aitken Lord Beaverbrook when he was alive. Now that I have learnt to know him better from his records I love him even more."

Whatever Beaverbrook and Joe Kennedy might have thought about how the other behaved as a father, it was Kennedy whose commitment and interests prevailed. He insisted on sharing with Beaverbrook his sons' political successes, as first Jack, then Bobby achieved high public office. While they were not Beaverbrook's sons, and while he may have lacked Joe Kennedy's capacity for parental pride, Beaverbrook found vicarious pleasure in helping his friend's sons succeed so spectacularly, a pleasure that surely reached its apogee the day Senator John F. Kennedy came to speak at Beaverbrook's university.

RFK COMES TO UNB

On the tenth anniversary of JFK's visit to the University of New Brunswick, brother Robert came. He was almost precisely the same age, 41, John had been when he had visited a decade before. Although still a new senator, it was no secret that RFK was getting ready to challenge for the presidency the following year. His visit therefore conveyed much the same sense of impending historical significance, only greater, for by now the Kennedy family phenomenon was more widely known. Forty Canadian newspapers, from the *Halifax Mail-Star* to the *Vancouver Sun*, covered the event. Like his brother, RFK had come to receive an honorary degree and give a speech. At convocation he was introduced by

the same University Orator, Professor Robert E. D. Cattley. In light of what transpired over the next eight months, there is both pathos and irony in the Orator's remarks:

> He is the second Kennedy whom it has been my privilege to present for this degree, and this is a memorable moment.
>
> The Kennedys are world figures. A dynastic aura is already forming around that brilliant and controversial family. And it envelopes our attractive visitor.
>
> A supremely youthful forty-one, he is the *non-pareil* of American youth. Tousle-haired, athletic, and venturesome, his every activity is exhaustively chronicled, whether he is shooting the rapids of an Idaho river, scaling the 14,000 ft. peak of Mt. Kennedy in Canada, or sailing the reef-studded waters of Penobscot Bay.
>
> His domestic life has a spontaneous appeal. Father of 10, the relentless press camera catches him romping with his younger fry, dealing with their animal pets, or playing that taxing Kennedy touch-football, his wife Ethel a valiant team-mate....
>
> There is an old Greek proverb: "Office will prove the man." To Robert Kennedy have fallen two great public offices. He is a member, very junior, of the United States Senate, and was before that a member, very prominent, of the President's cabinet. His record in

each has been full of promise. As a Senator he had within three weeks of his swearing-in introduced the first of several well-reasoned amendments, whereas his brothers waited, one five months, the other sixteen, to deliver their maiden speeches. As Attorney General he early outlived the stigma of nepotism and left an impressive record in the broad areas of civil rights, prison reform and immigration.

Such are not cloud but substance.

For higher goals he disclaims any present ambition. He can afford to. For it is salutary to remember that in 1972 the present Vice-President will be sixty-one, one in three of all American voters will be under 35, and Robert Francis Kennedy only 46.

Before referring to his script, Bobby endears himself to his audience with a piece of topical humour. Earlier that year (1967) General Charles de Gaulle, President of France, had visited Quebec and, with separatist feeling running high, had ended his farewell speech with a seeming call to arms to Quebec nationalists: "Vive le Quebec Libre." The incident had precipitated a diplomatic storm. Prime Minister Lester Pearson was outraged. RFK shows that he is aware of what has transpired. He says that, in preparing his remarks for this occasion, he had consulted a number of world leaders to ask how they thought he should begin, and one had suggested a no-miss salutation. It was "Vive New Brunswick Libre."

With that topical ad lib RFK assures his audience, as had JFK, that he knows where he is and who they are. Looking out on an arena filled to the rafters, he turns to his text and continues with a tribute to Lord Beaverbrook, who had died three years before, and to his son, Sir Max Aitken, himself now Chancellor of the University of New Brunswick.

...a no-miss salutation. It was "Vive New Brunswick Libre."

DIFFERENT PATHS OF A COMMON GOAL

Early in his speech RFK observes, "Lord Beaverbrook played a very important role in my brother's election in 1952 to the United States Senate." As though picking up from where his brother had left off ten years ago, he observes that much has changed for Canada and the United States in that period. It is quickly clear, however, that he intends to take his audience in a different direction, one less political, more spiritual. "Canada, like the United States, is a land of great wealth and of great enterprise. Canada, like the United States, is one of those tiny handful of nations confronted not with the crisis of physical survival, but with the dilemmas of modern affluence. And Canada, like the United States, is coming to realize that the accumulation of wealth will not fulfill the promise of our national lives—or the desires of our own human spirits."

With affluence comes effluence, both material and moral. Speaking of the United States, he says, "We have revolutionized our lives with electricity—but the power plants pollute our air. Our industry continues to grow, continues to swell the Gross National Product—but it also turns rivers into sewers, and lakes into swamps." Lest his audience be tempted to feel morally superior, however, he sets a clever rhetorical trap: "Just the other day I saw in an American newspaper a photograph of a woman, weeping outside the house that she lived in for years. It had been condemned as part of an urban renewal project. It was stark testimony to a system of remote and impersonal government. It is a picture we have seen in the United States for twenty years. But this photograph was taken in Canada."

"We have revolutionized our lives with electricity— but the power plants pollute our air. Our industry continues to grow, continues to swell the Gross National Product— but it also turns rivers into sewers, and lakes into swamps."

Sharing the burdens and benefits of prosperity, as Americans and Canadians do, means sharing "a common horizon" on the rest of the world—a turbulent and troubled world, a world undergoing a new kind of revolution. This revolution is a struggle for dignity in "societies where the individual is submerged in a desperate mass." There is nothing abstractly ideological about this revolution. It is rooted in social and economic struggle for self-sufficiency, for decent wages and living conditions, for medical services and education. "This is the world we confront today: a world which is an affront to our spirit, to the spirit of this University. For whatever political beliefs we hold, whatever our wish for the world of the future, there is to all men of goodwill a monstrous disproportion in our existence today—dieting while others starve, buying millions of cars each year while most of the world goes without shoes, islands of affluence in a sea of poverty."

Through jolting juxtapositions, RFK brings home to his listeners the imperatives inherent in such a practical revolution: "We cannot rest, apathetic and indifferent, prospering while others starve. We cannot have peaceful progress—if all around us nations and people are in chaos and are in agony." The only worthy response is to act in a manner consistent with the best of our heritage. "Throughout history, the boundaries of great empires have faded and have dissolved, their cities have fallen into decay, and their wealth has vanished. What remains for them is what they stood for, what they did for other people."

What, RFK asks, will endure for our own civilization, that of Canada and the U.S.? Not the wars we won or the wealth we accumulated, but whether we found a way out of the "terrible paradox that in an age of unbounded human possibility, men should hate and kill and want to destroy one another." Feeling the need for authority to strengthen his call for the tolerance that is a precondition of freedom and prosperity, RFK quotes two of his principal exemplars, Thomas Jefferson and John F. Kennedy. Hope may be found where his brother found it a decade ago: in the young. Here RFK employs a few lyrical phrases he had used the previous year in a speech to young South Africans in his Day of Affirmation address at Cape Town University. Youth, he said on that occasion, "is not a time of life, but a state of mind; a temper of the will; a quality of the imagination; a predominance of courage over timidity, of the appetite for adventure over the love of ease."

Drawing further on the South Africa speech, he raises and answers three objections that are likely to be brought against the response he advocates. First, that there is nothing one man or woman can do: "Few will have the greatness to bend history to itself; but each of us can work to change a small portion of events, and in the total of these acts will be written the history of this generation." Second, that idealism must bend before immediate necessity: "This ignores the realities of human faith and passion and belief; forces ultimately more powerful than all the calculations of economists and generals." Third is the spiritual inertia caused by our own comfortable lives. Here RFK could speak with personal moral authority. Born to affluence, he might well have chosen to "follow the easy and familiar paths of personal ambition and financial success." Instead, he chose a harder path, one that had already cost his brother his life and, less than a year later, would cost him his own. More than speech craft, it is the quality of Robert Kennedy's character that makes his oratory compelling.

His call to moral arms blends an appeal to Canadian pride with a plea for humanitarian action:

> You come from a nation whose Prime Minister holds a Nobel Prize for his work in bringing peace to a war-ravaged land; a nation whose work abroad has been a living testament to man's longing for peace;

His call to moral arms blends an appeal to Canadian pride with a plea for humanitarian action.

a land whose people have put their energy and their wisdom to the task of a world in which human freedom is enlarged and peace preserved. Now you must turn to the work of building a newer world—a world that will be better for the work that you do. And this you must do.

Albert Camus once said: "Perhaps we cannot prevent this world from being a world in which children suffer. But we can lessen the number of suffering children. And if you do not help us do this, who will do this?"

This is the question that the young graduates of this University must ask themselves. I am convinced of the answer.

The applause reverberated in the cavernous ice rink, and a host of young people waited for him outside to get his autograph and to touch him. As he climbed into the car that would take him to the airport, he shouted: "Come down and vote in the United States sometime."

It was the only speech Robert Kennedy would make in Canada. Ten years earlier Beaverbrook had written: "I find Bobby a most lively character with an exceedingly aggressive mind, well-balanced, clear in statement, powerful in argument, well-read and bound to do a great deal in life." Had he lived to hear his UNB speech Beaverbrook would have had confirmation of his assessment.

The climax comes at the very end, in a quotation from one of his favourite authors. He had discovered Camus after his brother John's death. In a search to find a philosophical context to reconcile his sense of despair with his need for action, he had read *The Stranger*, the *Notebooks*, and *Resistance, Rebellion, and Death*, and had had quotations from these books typed on index cards. The passage he used for his UNB address was one that he had copied himself into his daybook.

RFK seemed in his style of public address less conscious than his brother of a tradition of eloquence, but the facility with which he could enlist the wisdom of Aeschylus or Jefferson or Camus, among others, suggests he too was mindful of that tradition. Nor was it just on those occasions when he had a well-prepared text. His extemporaneous speech, from the back of a flatbed truck, in the freezing rain, to a predominantly black audience in Indianapolis on April 4, 1968, informing them of the assassination of Martin Luther King Jr., is both eloquent and profoundly moving, especially his from-memory quoting of Aeschylus: "In our sleep, pain which cannot forget falls drop by drop upon the heart until, in our own despair, against our will, comes wisdom through the awful grace of God."

Neither RFK nor JFK was a rafter-ringing orator, or wished to be. As John put it, "Those guys who can make the rafters ring with hokum—well, I guess that's O.K., but it keeps me from being an effective political speaker." Instead, the brothers combined sincerity of manner with speech texts that were beautifully crafted. In this regard the speeches they gave at the University of New Brunswick are typical of those they gave throughout their political careers. But as much as the UNB speeches bear out differences, they also demonstrate the brothers' shared talent for developing and delivering powerful messages. That they would make two of their finest speeches at a small university in Canada speaks eloquently to how seriously each took every speaking engagement.

❀❀❀❀❀

A TRADITION OF RHETORICAL ELOQUENCE

There are two questions addressed in this little book. The first is why did the Kennedy brothers, each on the verge of a run for the presidency of the United States and, as a consequence, husbanding time strategically, interrupt their hectic schedules to visit Fredericton, New Brunswick, where there was no possibility of political gain? The second question is why did they take time and care to prepare and deliver exceptionally fine speeches when a few words off the cuff would have served?

The answer to the first question, as I have tried to show, may be found in the extraordinary relationship between their father, Joseph P. Kennedy, and Max Aitken, Lord Beaverbrook. The answer to the second lies in an American tradition that the brothers inherited and made distinguished contributions to: a tradition for which there is no match in Canada or perhaps elsewhere in the English-speaking world, a tradition of rhetorical eloquence and elegance.

There are many reasons for this difference in national rhetorical traditions, and a thorough exploration of them lies well beyond the scope of my purpose here. Some of the difference is religious and some is secular. Radical Protestantism, with its emphasis on expounding the word of God and thereby fostering a tradition of soul-saving pulpit oratory, played a prominent part in the fashioning of American society, and thereby in the shaping of American political rhetoric. For Canada, by contrast, it was the combined traditions of the Roman Catholic and the Anglican churches that largely defined the more conservative and communitarian, and hence less charismatic, spirit of Canadian culture.

In the secular realm, a concomitant spirit of individualism was part and parcel of the American enlightenment ethos, born of the fact and the spirit of revolution, where right and wrong must be more categorically defined. In Canada the prevailing spirit was one of social evolution. As many have noted, the constitution of the United States promises each citizen "life, liberty, and the pursuit of happiness," while the British North America Act names as its more modest objective "peace, order, and good government." As one might expect, therefore, the rhetorical and oratorical traditions of the two countries reflect this difference. A communitarian culture suggests many voices speaking provisionally and conditionally; an individualistic zeitgeist permits a more authoritative style.

In consequence, from the beginning American orators in different spheres have been honoured, their speeches published and used as models. One thinks of Jonathan Edwards's "Sinners in the Hands of an Angry God" (1741), Patrick Henry's "Liberty or Death" (1775), Thomas Jefferson's "First Inauguration Address" (1801), Ralph Waldo Emerson's "The American Scholar" (1837), Abraham Lincoln's "Gettysburg Address" (1863), Booker T. Washington's "Atlanta Exposition Address" (1895), Franklin Delano Roosevelt's "First Inaugural Address" (1933), and the inspiring oratory of the Kennedy brothers and Martin Luther King Jr. in the second half of the twentieth century, and Barack Obama at the beginning of the twenty-first. Such speeches, much published and quoted, constitute a canon of eloquence and stand as proof of a reverence for oratory constructed on classical rhetoric.

This tradition finds its apotheosis in presidential inaugural and state-of-the-union addresses where, in addition to substantive content, the speeches are expected to serve as examples of rhetorical excellence. In contrast, the Canadian equivalent, the speech from the throne, requires the nation's leader, the prime minister, to speak not in his or her own voice but through the titular head of state, the governor-general. While normally well-crafted, such speeches have too much utilitarian cargo ever to rise to true eloquence, which always requires some passion and originality of expression on the part of the speaker.

U.S. presidents have a sense of speaking, not just to the audience listening, but to posterity. Hence they enlist talented wordsmiths to forge the telling phrase, the compelling image, the *mot juste*. This is as true of presidents who have themselves little natural eloquence as of those that do. In fact, the strength of the tradition is perhaps best observed when there is an obvious discrepancy between the innate verbal talents of the president and the elegance of the lines being delivered.

No one better combined natural eloquence with an appreciation for the value of the tradition of public eloquence than John F. Kennedy. In his inaugural address he gave proof of how well he had mastered the arts of rhetoric, arts he had been practising for many years. Early in his career he had considered himself a mediocre speaker. Someone who heard him said he spoke "in a voice somewhat scratchy and tensely high-pitched. . . . No trace of humour leavened his talk. Hardly diverging from his prepared text, he stood as if before a blackboard, addressing a classroom full of pupils who could be expected at any moment to become unruly." With the help of his family, and especially his father, Jack had honed his presentation skills and had become a superb communicator both in his formal addresses and in interactive press conferences.

His speech at the University of New Brunswick illustrates how seriously he took every speaking engagement, even one in a country of which he knew and would continue to know little. In 1957 he had received more than 2500 speaking invitations, and had accepted 144. That the University of New Brunswick would be the site of one of those is proof of JFK's immense regard for his father's friend, Lord Beaverbrook. That his speech should be so finely crafted and eloquently delivered is evidence of his devotion to the tradition of eloquence that American presidents, above all others, seek to honour.

Canada has had its fair share of gifted talkers (none better than Beaverbrook himself), and a goodly number of effective orators. What it has not had is a tradition of celebrating and honouring eloquent and original speeches. Only recently has rhetoric become a discipline of language closely studied in Canadian universities, and, by comparison with the multitude of collections of great American speeches, Canada has produced to date scant few. Some might look for the cause of this discrepancy in the difference between a parliamentary and a congressional system of government: the one rewarding sharp riposte, the other favouring the oratorical occasion. Others might point to the much longer practice of celebrating and studying the verbal arts in the United States, especially its national literature, when compared to Canada whose rich vein of literature has been honoured for only the past half-century. Still others might point to the imperial nature of the American presidency as the motive power of the tradition. Whatever the cause, there is no denying the existence in the United States of a powerful tradition of public eloquence of which American presidents, and presidential hopefuls are expected to be exemplars, and of which the Kennedy brothers consummately were.

CONVOCATION ADDRESS

by

John Fitzgerald Kennedy

United States Senator

Tuesday, October 8th, 1957

at the

THE UNIVERSITY

OF NEW BRUNSWICK

Fredericton, NB, Canada

‘

GOOD FENCES MAKE GOOD NEIGHBORS

It is a very great honor

for a New Englander like myself to come to this city and institution which represent so impressive a link between the New World and the Old.
I am most grateful for the degree which you have seen fit to award me and am most honored to receive it at the hands of your distinguished Chancellor, Lord Beaverbrook. For Lord Beaverbrook

is today, as he has been for several decades, one of the outstanding figures of the English speaking world, a man whose multiple careers and talents leave continuing imprints on our times.

As the faithful Cerberus of imperial interests, as the first magnate of Fleet Street, as one of the genuinely skillful controversialists of our day, as a historian cast in the mould of a modern Plutarch, as a benefactor of learning and culture—one cannot fail to give him a many-salvoed salute! Nor can any American forget the supremely gifted services which Lord Beaverbrook rendered to the cause of Freedom in the 2nd World War in partnership with Sir Winston Churchill. Lord Beaverbrook's views and editorial declarations may often be at odds with our own individual attitudes, but one is grateful for the candor, and clear formulation of his opinions, which often act as powerful antidotes and stimulants even when they do not entirely persuade. Recently Lord Beaverbrook has published the first of a new trilogy of volumes illuminating the public events in which he has played so central a part. Many of us have read already his pungent pages of the age of Lloyd George, which are filled with fresh insights, revealing vignettes, and striking recreations of important historical episodes. In this venture too Lord Beaverbrook shares the bold vision of human understanding, and inexhaustible curiosity of his friend Sir Winston. We are fortunate that we may expect at least two more volumes on the Ages of Baldwin and Churchill from his pen. By his life and efforts he has served as a bridge between the old and new worlds, as a link between the golden past and the uncertain present.

While I am grateful for the personal satisfaction thus accorded me, I know that this is simply another demonstration of the continued strengthening of the common ties that bind together Canada and the United States, New Brunswick and Massachusetts: ties of history, ties of kinship and ties of an inseparable destiny. Both New Brunswick and Massachusetts border on the Atlantic Ocean, with rich maritime and fishing traditions. Both were instrumental in the formation of their nations, New Brunswick being one of the four provinces united in the Dominion in 1867, and Massachusetts being one of the 13 united to form the American Union of 1787. Throughout the history of Massachusetts, a large proportion of its residents have traced their origins to New Brunswick and the other Canadian provinces. Indeed, of all the many residents of my state of Massachusetts who were born outside of the United States, a much larger percentage—

more than one out of four—were born in Canada than in any other country.

New Brunswick, too, has many residents who can trace their ancestry back to the United States and Massachusetts—although in many instances this relates to an unhappy period in the history of our two countries. Following the Revolutionary War the so-called Tories who had remained loyal to the British Crown did not fare well in America. The freshly victorious colonists were proud in their new independence, and angry at those who had not joined them during the bitter years of struggle. Their patience and tolerance, I am afraid, were limited—and so harshly were some Tories treated that they were forced to flee the country. One of the favorite havens of refuge for those coming from Massachusetts was the province of New Brunswick.

Incidentally, when the United States in cooler times offered amnesty to these exiles, one Charles Wentworth Upham, born in New Brunswick of parents who had fled from Boston, returned to the ancestral home of Massachusetts and settled in Salem. His distinguished career included service as President of the Massachusetts Senate and as one of my early predecessors in the Massachusetts delegation to the United States House of Representatives, and interestingly enough by marrying the sister of Oliver Wendell

Holmes, Sr., this native of New Brunswick became an uncle of one of the most distinguished sons of our Commonwealth and one of the most famous of our nation's Supreme Court's Justices.

At the moment we see and hear much about a "new chapter" in the relations between the United States and Canada. Unquestionably the new Canadian Government under Prime Minister Diefenbaker has received a mandate to explore means by which Canada may renew a closer trade connection with Great Britain and take a new compass bearing on international economic policies. But in reading the statements made by your Prime Minister on several recent occasions, both in this country and in the United States, it is quite apparent that the main outlines of Canadian policy are but little altered. Both of our peoples delude themselves if they believe that there is some new and previously unexplored line of policy which Canada can now explore. It does no service either, to suppose that Canada has a closed option between a "pro-British" and a "pro-American" approach to foreign policy and trade. Canada can neither be an extension of the Cornish coastline nor is she a mere northern vestibule to the United States. Canada has achieved a national strength and prestige which simply does not allow any portrayal of the country as an appendage of either Great Britain or the United States. To be sure, Canada has some special links with each of these two English-speaking nations, but it possesses most certainly a national destiny of its own to which it is well and timely to give foremost recognition.

The United States and Canada are more than ever continental partners. Not only do they share Atlantic and Pacific coastlines; they now also have a long common coast along the St. Lawrence Seaway, which is opening up new maritime centers on both sides of the border. Natural conditions decree that we share common interests in hydro-electric power, natural gas, high sea fisheries. Our defense perimeters have merged all the way to the Arctic. Our agricultural economies have common characteristics and weaknesses born of abundance. This common heritage gives strength to both of our countries, but we must frankly concede that the very closeness of our interests and national aspirations have recently brought new frictions and irritations to the surface. The resilience and buoyancy of our two economies have been accompanied by under-standable collisions and misunderstandings.

For example, our natural resources should not be neatly compartmentalized nationally. We must soon resolve the disputes which have arisen over the uses to which some of the waters of the Columbia, Yukon, and St. John Rivers are to be put. There remain some unresolved questions about the St. Lawrence Seaway, especially regarding the level of tolls. Fisheries have been a classical issue in the relations between our two countries, whereas the methods by which we dispose of agriculture surpluses have become a new source of tension. The deep penetration of American venture capital and business management into Canadian enterprises in such sectors as mining and fuels has aroused natural fears among Canadians. And there are more than a few Canadians who are appalled that the hopes for a distinctively national cultural tradition are being suffocated by a loud cacophony south of the border.

These are examples of the types of tensions which suggest that we should improve the machinery of joint consultation and management. A small beginning is being made in the business sphere by the committee on economic relations established by the National Planning Association under the chairmanship of former Ambassador R. Douglas Stuart and Mr. R. M. Fowler of Montreal. This committee will make special inquiry into the questions of U. S. domination in Canadian enterprise and the dumping of agricultural surpluses. In my judgment, however, our two nations should devise far better permanent consultative channels so that each new problem does not have to be dealt with on an ad hoc and individual emergency basis. Fortunately, our two governments are able to carry on a frank dialogue and you have been most ably represented by men such as Mr. St. Laurent, Mr. Pearson, Mr. Howe and their successors, Mr. Diefenbaker and Dr. Smith. But, in addition to "summit meetings," we should make sure that our regular and standing organs of consultation keep abreast, in structure and outlook, with the new currents of change.

But new or reorganized agencies are of little help unless we simultaneously achieve an understanding on basic issues. Most important, we should guard against an outbreak of mutual economic retaliation and restrictionism which amount to little more than scapegoat hunting and provide at best transitory defense. If the Canadian Government is in fact able, as intimated at the recent Commonwealth Conferences at London and Mt. Tremblant, to divert a larger portion of its trade to Britain, this should not be occasion for the United States to launch a new program of economic retaliation and harassment.

Likewise, I feel that the Canadian Government would gain little by approaching the matter of American business influence in too narrow a context. There may be good grounds for requiring fuller financial statements by U. S.

businesses of operations in Canada and possibly some other limitations, but this is quite different from writing into Law a long and harassing set of controls. The Canadian free enterprise system has been remarkably well balanced and liberal in recent years; all Americans envy its success when confronted with premium dollars and the record of inflation control it has made. It would be a pity to rigidify the Canadian economy merely for the sake of breaking lances with a phantom American colonialism. In return, American businessmen, with substantial investments in Canada should be required by the dictates of self-preservation, if not simple equity, to increase the participation of Canadian money and personnel in the development of Canadian resources. A chain reaction of economic reprisal would greatly set back our relations without measurably helping even the narrowly conceived interests of either nation.

Today, if the United States and Canada, with their common language, common history, common economic and political interests and other close ties cannot live peacefully with one another, then what hope is there for the rest of the world? We have a responsibility to demonstrate to all peoples everywhere that peaceful and stable existence, by powerful countries side by side, can remain a permanent reality in today's troubled world.

Today, for example, the Arabs and the Israelis would do well to recall the tense relations and boundary disputes which divided the United States and Canada over a century ago—of how finally the Webster-Ashburton Treaty of 1842 was devised to settle these differences, with some concessions by both parties—and of how unpopular that treaty was on both sides of the line, with both Mr. Webster of Massachusetts and Lord Ashburton being repeatedly denounced for having sacrificed the rights of their people. (Indeed, Webster and Ashburton finally convinced the Senate and Parliament respectively, it is said, only after each had used a different map to pretend that he had in reality cheated the other.) And yet the peace and prosperity to both countries flowing from that much abused settlement for more than a century have been worth several thousand times as much as the value of all the territory that was in dispute.

I do not mean to imply that the relations between our two nations are so close as to encourage domination or subservience. This has not been a case where in terms of the old saying "familiarity breeds contempt." On the contrary, a co-operative friendship of such meaning and solidarity permits a full and frank discussion of issues of mutual interest, even when that discussion may jar sensitive ears on the other side of the border. Your Prime Minister, I believe, has done well to remind both countries of the issues and potential areas of conflict that our two countries must not neglect. A friendship such as ours, moreover encourages healthy competition in international trade, it requires that neither take the other for granted in international politics.

"Good fences," reads a poem by one of our most distinguished New England poets, Robert Frost, "make good neighbours." Canada and the United States have carefully maintained the good fences that help make them good neighbours.

In the final analysis, the elimination of these various tensions and misunderstandings on both sides of the border cannot depend upon any treaty or mechanical formula or ancient statute, but must rely upon the wisdom, understanding and ability of the leaders and officials of our two nations, upon the thought and effort they are willing to give to clearing up these misunderstandings. It will require in both Canada and America political leaders of patience, tact and foresight—dedicated, responsible men who can look beyond the problems of the next election to see the problems of the next generation. Where, in the future, are those leaders to come from? Primarily from the University of New Brunswick and the University of Massachusetts, from all of the colleges and educational institutions of our two nations. In the long run, it is upon these colleges and the type of graduates they produce that the continuation of Canadian-American friendship depends.

I do not say that our international relations, or our political and public life, should be completely turned over to college-trained experts who ignore public opinion. Nor would I adopt for my own country the provision from the Belgian Constitution of 1893 giving three votes instead of one to college graduates (at least not until more Democrats go to college). Nor do I suggest that the University of New Brunswick be given a seat in Parliament as our William and Mary College was once represented in the Virginia House of Burgesses.

But I do urge that each of you, regardless of your chosen occupation, consider entering the field of politics at some stage in your career, that you offer to the political arena, and to the critical problems of our society which are decided therein —including the delicate problems of Canadian-American cooperation—the benefits of the talents which society has helped to develop in you. I ask you to decide, as Goethe put it, whether you will be an anvil—or a hammer. The formal phases of the "anvil" stage will soon be completed for many of you, though hopefully you will continue to absorb still more in the years ahead. The question

now is whether you are to be a hammer—
whether you are to give to the world in which you
are reared and educated the broadest possible
benefits of that education.

This is a great university, the University of
New Brunswick. Its establishment and continued
functioning, like that of all great universities, has
required considerable effort and expenditure.
I cannot believe that all of this was undertaken
merely to give the school's graduates an economic
advantage in the life struggle. "A university," said
Professor Woodrow Wilson, "should be an organ
of memory for the state for the transmission of
its best traditions. Every man sent out from a
university should be a man of his nation, as well
as a man of his time." And Prince Bismarck was
even more specific—one third of the students of
German universities, he once stated, broke down
from overwork; another third broke down from
dissipation; and the other third ruled Germany.
(I leave it to each of you to decide which category
you fall in.)

But if you are to be among the rulers of
your land, from alderman to prime minister, if
you are willing to enter the abused and neglected
profession of politics, then let me tell you—as one
who is familiar with the political world—that our
profession in all parts of the world stands
in serious need of the fruits of your education.

We do not need political scholars whose education has been so specialized as to exclude them from participation in current events—men like Lord John Russell, of whom QueenVictoria once remarked that he would be a better man if he knew a third subject—but he was interested in nothing but the Constitution of 1688 and himself. No, what we need are men who can ride easily over broad fields of knowledge and recognize the mutual dependence of our two worlds, men like my nation's Thomas Jefferson, whom a contemporary described as "A gentleman of 32, who could calculate an eclipse, survey an estate, tie an artery, plan an edifice, try a case, break a horse, dance a minuet, and play the violin".

I realize that politics has become one of our most neglected, our most abused and our most ignored professions. It ranks low on the occupational list of a large share of the population; and its chief practitioners are rarely well or favorably known. No education, except finding your way around a smoke-filled room, is considered necessary for political success. "Don't teach my boy poetry," a mother recently wrote the headmaster of Eton, "he's going to stand for Parliament." The worlds of politics and scholarship have indeed drifted apart.

But it is here, I repeat, that the foundations for future Canadian-American relations must be laid, here in this citadel of learning, from which you can take with you upon graduation all the accumulated knowledge and inspiration you may need to face the future. I am assuming, of course, that you are taking something with you, that you do not look upon this university as Dean Swift regarded Oxford. Oxford, he said, was truly a great seat of learning; for all freshmen who entered were required to bring some learning with them in order to meet the standards of admission —but no senior, when he left the university, ever took any learning away; and thus it steadily accumulated.

We want from you not the sneers of the cynics or the despair of the faint-hearted. Of that we already have an abundance. We ask that you bring enlightenment, vision, and illumination to a troubled world, where the rock of our two nations' friendship must always stand firm.

In his book, "One Man's America," Alistair Cooke tells the story which well illustrates this point. On the 19th of May 1780, as he describes it, in Hartford, Connecticut the skies at noon turned from blue to gray and by mid-afternoon had blackened over so densely that, in the religious age, men fell on their knees and begged a final blessing before the end came. The Connecticut House of Representatives was in session.

And as some men fell down in the darkened chamber and others clamored for an immediate adjournment, the Speaker of the House, one Colonel Davenport, came to his feet. And he silenced the din with these words: "The Day of Judgment is either approaching—or it is not. If it is not, there is no cause for adjournment. If it is, I choose to be found doing my duty. I wish therefore that candles may be brought."

Students of the University of New Brunswick, we who are here today concerned with the dark and difficult task ahead ask once again that you bring candles to illuminate our way.

CONVOCATION ADDRESS

by

Robert Francis Kennedy

United States Senator

Thursday, October 12th, 1967

at the

THE UNIVERSITY

OF NEW BRUNSWICK

Fredericton, NB, Canada

DIFFERENT PATHS
OF A COMMON GOAL

I THINK IT'S MARVELOUS
that we're all here today.
I think it shows how attached you are to the University,
that those of you who are here today are not watching
television or listening to the radio
and listening to the baseball game.
And I'm very appreciative.
All I can do is promise you that my speech will be
short. But I'm very grateful to come here.

Max Aitken has been a long-time friend of the Kennedy family, and he was a great friend of President Kennedy. And I have long been an admirer of his, as I was of his father, who has so much to do with this University, and who was a great friend of my father's, and also a great friend of President Kennedy.

There were more people, I think, from New Brunswick and representing the Maritime areas in the State of Massachusetts than any other part of the world.

And it's the first time it's been disclosed but I think Lord Beaverbrook played a very important role in my brother's election in 1952 to the United States Senate. He took an active interest and I think that he and those of you who were friendly at that time made it a matter of some importance to your relatives in Massachusetts to vote for John Kennedy. So we're very grateful.

It is always an honor to receive a degree from a great university. But this is a day of special pride for me. It was just ten years ago, at your Fall Convocation, that John Kennedy was presented with an honorary Doctors of Law degree at this same ceremony.

Much has changed in the last ten years. And at this University, your Chancellor, Lord Beaverbrook, has gone. But his contributions to the Province of New Brunswick, and to this University, remain. The art gallery; the play-house; the town hall auditoriums, have enriched the cultural life of New Brunswick. And the Library, the Gymnasium, the Pool that Max Aitken opened today are going to make great contributions and continue to make great contributions to this University, the people of New Brunswick and to the people of Canada.

Lord Beaverbrook was a man of firm conviction and he expressed those convictions forcefully. But whatever one's disagreements were with individual positions that he might have taken, no one will deny that he left a rewarding legacy to the Province of New Brunswick—to its University—and I think beyond that, to all English-speaking people all over the globe. I think the world is better that Lord Beaverbrook lived.

Your nation has also changed much in the last ten years. Your natural resources have been fused with a great outpouring of energy by the people of Canada, to create one of the most vibrant and successful economies of the whole world. Industrial production has increased by more than 50 per cent; you exchange more than 20 billion dollars worth of goods with the rest of the world; and you have fueled this growth with new sources of energy—including the advanced nuclear plants at Rolphton and Douglas Point.

But if Canada—and the United States—have changed in the last ten years, these changes have dramatized the links that bind us together. For Canada, like the United States, is a land of great wealth and of great enterprise. Canada, like the United States, is one of those tiny handful of nations confronted not with the crisis of physical survival, but with the dilemmas of modern affluence. And Canada, like the United States, is coming to realize that the accumulation of material wealth will not fulfill the promise of our national lives—or the desires of our own human spirits.

We in the United States are sometimes thought of as the most affluent of all the nations of the globe. You in Canada are rapidly advancing to the same equal peak of material prosperity. But we have found, in our own country, that the statistics of modern progress perhaps count the wrong things; for the forms of the new wealth seem to destroy as many pleasures as they bring.

We have revolutionized our lives with electricity—but the power plants pollute our air. Our industry continues to grow, continues to swell the Gross National Product—but it also turns rivers into sewers, and lakes into swamps.

And as our wealth increases, so also does the pace and the complexity of our national existence. We crowd into cities; we spill out into chaotic, and unplanned suburbs; and link the two with ribbons of concrete, desecrating the landscape and poisoning the air. We confront a society composed of giants—of huge, impersonal corporations, bureaucratic universities, centralized government, in which the solitary, individual man too often goes unrecognized and unheard.

But as all these problems come to the United States, so do they come to all of the industrialized nations of the world in the larger society that we call the West; and so they will and so they are now confronting Canada.

Just the other day I saw in an American newspaper a photograph of a woman, weeping outside the house that she lived in for years. It had been condemned as part of an urban renewal project. It was stark testimony to a system of remote and impersonal government. It is a picture we have seen in the United States for twenty years. But this photograph was taken in Canada.

Thus we are destined to share the burdens as well as the benefits of modern life. We share in the shape of our societies; with the sure knowledge that all our great common enterprises will come to little if we cannot rebuild and re-enforce the importance of the individual man; to gain for ourselves and for our children the opportunity to live as the Greeks defined happiness: "the exercise of vital powers along the lines of excellence in a life affording them scope."

And even as we share this crisis of prosperity within our two nations, so do we look out upon a common horizon abroad. For we face a troubled and a turbulent world; a world full of a new kind of revolution.

This is not a revolution of ideology. It is a revolution for individual dignity, in societies where the individual is submerged in a desperate mass. It is a revolution for self-sufficiency, in societies which have been forced to rely on another, stronger nation—our nation—for everything from their manufactured goods to their education. And it is a revolution to bring hope to their children; the generation of young people who live in lands where the average wage may be 75 cents a day, as in Latin America, or $100 a year, as in Africa. These are children who live without doctors and without medicine. Seven out of ten children in thousands of Latin American villages die before they reach their first birthday and half of the people who are buried in Latin America each year are under the age of four. These are the children who, if they live, face only the prospect of wretched, weary lives; lives of endless toil, without joy, without purpose, and without hope.

This is the world that we confront today: a world which is an affront to our spirit, to the spirit of this University. For whatever political beliefs we hold, whatever our wish for the world of the future, there is to all men of goodwill a monstrous disproportion in our existence today—dieting while others starve, buying millions of cars each year while most of the world goes without shoes, islands of affluence in a sea of poverty.

So we must recognize what we must do—and what we cannot do. We cannot rest, apathetic and indifferent, prospering while others starve. We cannot have peaceful progress—if all around us nations and people are in chaos and are in agony.

But more than this, we must act to honor the best within our heritage. Throughout history, the boundaries of great empires have faded and have dissolved, their cities have fallen into decay, and their wealth has vanished.

What remains for them is what they stood for, what they did for other people. What remains is the contribution that they made to the unity and to the knowledge, to the understanding and to the compassion of man. What remains is what they added to the hopes and the well-being of human civilization and to its hopes for the future.

What will endure of our own civilization, of Canada and of the United States, will not be the wars that we won, the weapons that we built, or the wealth that we accumulated. It will be what we can accomplish of the hope of a great political philosopher, Thomas Jefferson, who said, that "we are pointing the way to struggling nations who wish like us to emerge from their own tyrannies also"—not only political tyranny, but the despots of poverty and of fear and of ignorance. It will be whether we can break out of the terrible paradox that in an age of unbounded human possibility, men should hate and kill and want to destroy one another.

For we must dissolve the attitudes which permit men to indulge those passions which keep the world in constant conflict. There have been more than seventy wars since the end of World War II: yet this chaos has not induced us to make much progress in reducing our capacity for nuclear destruction, which could make each momentary crisis the last crisis for all mankind, and we cannot do this by ourselves. Yet we can show increased understanding for the fears and the suspicions of others and take occasional risks in the name of peace in preference to the monumental risks in mounting arms.

Nor is the peace we seek mere inaction or the absence of war. "Peace," said President Kennedy, "is a process—a way of solving problems." Thus peace for us means building new forms of political and economic institutions, which the smallness and the terror of our whole world requires that we do.

But all of this commitment—in the peace and the progress of the world—also requires restraint, and it also requires understanding. For we cannot impose any rigid pattern, any single solution, on the diverse peoples of the world. Nations, like men, often march to the beat of different drummers; it is our role to help those nations achieve their own goals of political justice, national independence, and increasing human freedom—not to condition the help we have to offer on their allegiance to our own political lights.

These tasks—this commitment—this restraint—are awesome challenges in the years ahead. And there are those who question whether the energy and the will to meet these challenges is present in our land. Our answer, in my judgment, is to rely on youth—the world's hope. The world demands the qualities of youth. This is not a time of life, but a state of mind; a temper of the will; a quality of imagination; the predominance of courage over timidity, of the appetite for adventure over the love of ease.

Each nation has different obstacles and different goals, shaped by the vagaries of history and of experience. Yet as I talk to young people around the world I am impressed not by the diversity but by the closeness of their goals, their concerns, their values and their hopes for the future. I have seen students in South Africa, risking position and daring imprisonment against the awesome power of a garrison state. In Peru and Chile, I have seen students leaving the civilization of their university and of the city, to the danger and the disease and the squalor of the countryside, seeking justice and progress for the peasants who have never shared in the life of their country.

And in this task, the youth of Canada have a vital role to play. For you are among the few nations whose youth has been educated, and who can teach others the skills they need to lead lives of dignity and purpose. Canada stands, with the United States, with Europe, with Japan, in that small group of lands which do not fight a daily battle simply to stay alive.

You of Canada's younger generation have already begun this work. Through the Canadian University Service Overseas—an inspiration for our Peace Corps—more than 900 Canadians serve abroad, helping to teach the peoples of Africa, and Asia, and Latin America—just as the Company of

Young Canadians is working here in your own land. But much more needs to be done—and among your students are thousands who can bring hope into lands that know none.

But there are dangers in this commitment—and there are dangers that you must face and there are dangers that must be overcome. First, is the danger of futility; the belief that there is nothing that one man or one woman can do against the enormous array of the world's ills—against misery and against ignorance, against injustice or against violence. Yet many of the world's great movements, of thought and of action, have flowed from the work of a single man. A young Italian explorer discovered the new world, a young general extended an empire from Macedonia to the borders of the earth and a young woman reclaimed the territory of France. It was the 32 year-old Thomas Jefferson who proclaimed that all men are created equal.

"Give me a place to stand, and I can move the world," said Archimedes. These men moved the world, and so can we all. Few will have the greatness to bend history to itself; but each of us can work to change a small portion of events, and in the total of all these acts will be written the history of this generation. Each time a man stands up for an ideal, or acts to improve the lot of others, or strikes out against injustice, he sends forth a

tiny ripple of hope, and crossing each other
from a million different centers of energy and
daring, those ripples build a current which can
sweep down the mightiest walls of oppression
and resistance.

The second great danger is that of exped-
iency; of those who say that hopes and beliefs
must bend before immediate necessity. Of course,
if we would act effectively we must deal with the
world as it is. We must get things done.

But if there was one thing that President
Kennedy stood for that touched the most
profound feelings of young people all over the
globe, it was the belief that idealism, high
aspirations and deep convictions are not
incompatible with the most practical and efficient
of programs—that there is no basic inconsistency
between ideals and realistic possibilities—no
separation between the deepest desires of heart
and mind and the rational application of human
effort to human problems. It is not realistic or
hard-headed to solve problems and to take action
unguided by ultimate moral aims and moral
values. It is thoughtless folly. For it ignores the
realities of human faith and passion and belief;
forces ultimately more powerful than all the
calculation of economists and of generals. Of
course to adhere to standards, to idealism, to
vision, in the face of immediate dangers takes

courage and self-confidence. But we also know that only those who dare to fail greatly, can achieve greatly.

For the fortunate nations, like Canada and the United States, the third great danger is comfort; the temptation to follow the easy and familiar paths of personal ambition and financial success so grandly spread before those who have the privilege of an education. But that is not the road that history has marked out for us. There is a Chinese curse which says, "May he live in interesting times." Like it or not we live in interesting times. They are times of danger and they are times of uncertainty; but they are also open to the creative energy of man, more open than at any other time in this history of mankind. And everyone here will ultimately be judged, and more importantly, will ultimately judge himself, on the effort that he has contributed to building a new world society and the extent to which his ideals and his goals have shaped that effort.

You come from a nation whose Prime Minister holds a Nobel Prize for his work in bringing peace to a war-ravaged land; a nation whose work abroad has been a living testament to man's longing for peace; a land whose people have put their energy and their wisdom to the task of a world in which human freedom is enlarged, and peace preserved. Now you must turn to the work of building a newer world—a world which will be better for the work that you do. And this you must do.

Albert Camus once said:

"Perhaps we cannot prevent this world from being a world in which children suffer. But we can lessen the number of suffering children. And if you do not help us do this, who will do this?"

This is the question that the young graduates of this University must ask themselves. I am convinced of the answer.

✿✿✿✿✿

Lord Beaverbrook
and the Kennedys

Research Notes and References

Notes arising from the Preface of this book.

Page *xiii*

"two of only three they made in Canada"

The third speech was made by President Kennedy to the Canadian Houses of Parliament when he visited Canada in 1961.

Actually, JFK had made a second visit to Canada in the fall of 1957 when he took part in a debate at Hart House, University of Toronto. Opposing Kennedy was a very young Stephen Lewis, later to become Canada's ambassador to the United Nations. The following is the summary taken from my commonplace book, of a telephone conversation I had with Stephen Lewis on this subject on 9 June 2006.

> Spoke by phone today with Stephen Lewis about his recollection of the debate at Hart House in the fall of 1957 (November 14) where John F. Kennedy took part as a guest speaking from the floor, as was the Hart House tradition. The resolution was "Has the United States failed in its responsibilities as a world leader?" SL had spoken for the motion, JFK against. As was usual at Hart House, the guest's side won, but this time by an unusually narrow margin, 204 to 194. Kennedy's own performance, sticking closely to notes, had been rather poor. He seemed not in his element.
> It was the first debate at Hart House that women had been permitted to attend. After the debate the participants had retired to the warden's room for a chat with Kennedy. SL was struck with how "ideologically flexible" JFK was. When SL asked him how come someone who came from a life of privilege was a Democrat, he replied, "Because I was born in Massachusetts." SL said, "Does that mean if you had been born in Rhode Island you would be a Republican?" to which Kennedy replied, "Oh yes, absolutely."

❁❁❁❁❁

"Out of all these [British-American meetings] I have no re-collection whatsoever except the dynamism of Lord Beaverbrook. He was a power house with regard to what could be done and what had to be done."

Robert Beitzell, *The Uneasy Alliance: America, Britain, and Russia, 1941-43* (Knopf, 1972) p. 20.

Page 2

From that point on Beaverbrook . . . ensured favourable coverage
for the American ambassador.
David E. Koskoff, *Joseph P. Kennedy: A Life and Times* (Prentice-Hall, 1974),
p. 125.

When this information proved accurate, it was a boost not only
for British forces but also to Beaverbrook's standing with the
Churchill government.
Anne Chisholm and Michael Davie, *Beaverbrook: A Life* (Hutchinson, 1992),
p. 374.

In one of Lord Beaverbrook's books . . . *My Early Life* (Fredericton:
Brunswick Press, 1965), p 18.

Page 3

Thus, Beaverbrook concluded, "Nothing is so bad as consistency."
Lord Beaverbrook, *Success* (McClelland & Stewart, 1921), p. 101.

Page 4

Yet he sometimes ridiculed Churchill behind his back, calling him,
among other things, a terrible bore.
Amanda Smith, ed., *Hostage to Fortune: The Letters of Joseph P. Kennedy*
(Viking, 2001), p. 557.

Early in the war, when things were not going well for Churchill,
Beaverbrook even tested support (and found it virtually non-existent)
for his own chances of replacing him.
Chisholm and Davie, pp. 439-41. For a vivid, firsthand account of
Beaverbrook's hostility towards Churchill, see Averell W. Harriman and Elie
Abel, *Special Envoy to Churchill and Stalin, 1941-1946* (Random House,
1976), pp. 206-8.

"He couldn't resist seducing men the way he seduced women.
And once a man was seduced by him, he was finished."
Chisholm and Davie, p. 403.

Beaverbrook treated everyone close to him "with a mixture of charm, courtesy and ruthlessness."

Ibid., p. 9.

Nevertheless, in old age Kennedy wrote letters to only two friends, and Beaverbrook was one of them. The other friend was Enrico Galeazzi at the Vatican.

Smith, p. 520.

Kennedy in bootlegging during Prohibition, Beaverbrook through ruthless dealings in amassing shares for corporate mergers in Canada.

See Smith, pp. 107-9, on Joe Kennedy's involvement in the alcohol distribution trade; see Chisholm and Davie, pp. 66-8, for an account of Beaverbrook's part in the Canada Cement affair. In *Profits and Politics: Beaverbrook and the Gilded Age of Canadian Finance* (University of Toronto Press, 1996), Gregory P. Marchildon depicts Beaverbrook as a master financial manipulator who took full advantage of the freer investment laws of the Laurier era but did not profit excessively, and who engaged in less stock watering than the average merger of the time.

He wanted the United States to become a kind of giant Switzerland: well defended but neutral, and solely geared towards making money, not war.

For a fuller articulation of his views, see Joseph Kennedy's 1951 speech "Disentanglement," reprinted in *Readings in American Foreign Policy, 2nd Edition,* eds. Robert A. Goldwin and Harry M. Clor (Oxford University Press, 1971), pp. 162-9.

Page 5

A top advisor to Anthony Eden summarized the enmity when he noted, "Ambassador Kennedy is engaged in defeatist propaganda with Beaverbrook."

John Harvey, ed., *The Diplomatic Diaries of Oliver Harvey, 1937-1940* (Clear-Type Press, 1970), p. 326.

Page 6

"For a fellow who didn't want this war to touch your country or mine," he wrote to Beaverbrook, "I have had rather a bad dose—Joe dead, Billy Hartington dead, my son Jack in the naval hospital. I have had brought home to me very personally what I saw for all the mothers and fathers of the world."

Edward J. Renehan, Jr., *The Kennedys at War* (Doubleday, 2002), p. 311.

In all, Max flew 161 operational missions, saw action
throughout the Battle of Britain, and was credited with shooting down
16 German planes.
Lewis Chester and Jonathan Fenby, *The Fall of the House of Beaverbrook*
(Andre Deutsch, 1979), pp. 31-2.

Page 7

. . . as he "waited each night for Max's return from the skies where
London was saved and he himself had been translated into another
being."
Michael Foot, "The Case for Beelzebub," in *Debts of Honour*
(Davis Poynter Limited, 1980), p. 111.

Beaverbrook, he wrote in his diary, "didn't talk like his old self. He
talked as a Minister of the Churchill Government should, I suppose,
and seemed to be doing his best to sell me on the idea that things were
still all right."
Smith, p. 445.

To this end, he presented Roosevelt with rare gifts, including an original
Kipling manuscript. Chisholm and Davie, p. 444. . . . and also aimed his
considerable charm at the president's wife and daughter.
Doris Kearns Goodwin, *No Ordinary Time: Franklin and Eleanor Roosevelt;
The Home Front in World War II* (Simon & Schuster, 1994), p. 438.

In 1936, Beaverbrook was among a number of London-based
businessmen who helped William Randolph Hearst fund a smear
campaign against Roosevelt.
William E. Kinsella, Jr., *Leadership in Isolation: FDR and the Origins of the
Second World War* (Schenkman Publishing, 1978), p. 87.

Hearst had taken this promise as an attack aimed squarely at him.
Rodney P. Carlisle, *Hearst and the New Deal: The Progressive as
Reactionary* (Garland Publishing, 1979), pp. 93-4.

"This is for Hearst."
W. A. Swanberg, *Citizen Hearst: A Biography of William Randolph Hearst*
(Scribner's, 1961), p. 475.

. . . the Assistant Secretary of State, Sumner Welles, quickly confirmed
Dodd's suspicions.
Conrad Black, *Franklin Delano Roosevelt: Champion of Freedom*
(Public Affairs, 2003), p. 16.

Page 8

Increasingly, Roosevelt felt he could no longer rely on his ambassador.
Michael R. Beschloss, *Kennedy and Roosevelt: The Uneasy Alliance* (W.W. Norton, 1980), p. 16.

At a London dinner party, he bragged to friends that he could put "twenty-five million Catholic votes behind Wendell Willkie to throw Roosevelt out."
William Stevenson, *A Man Called Intrepid: The Secret War* (Harcourt Brace Jovanovich, 1976), p. 149.

Later that night, Kennedy further told Beaverbrook of a plot that he and Henry Luce had devised against the President.
Renehan, p. 170.

A long-time Republican supporter and a self-made man, Luce despised FDR.
Conrad Black insists that Luce was an "enlightened Republican" who, far from hating Roosevelt, supported him passionately in his move towards Anglo-American cooperation (p. 590). Black, however, is alone in this position. Biographers of Luce make it clear that he was an anti-New Dealer who used his media influence to create, support, and bolster the Willkie candidacy. See for example Robert E. Herzstein, *Henry R. Luce: A Political Portrait of the Man Who Created the American Century* (Scribner's, 1994), pp. 153-4.

What Luce would not have been so happy about, had he ever found out, was that Clare likely knew of Kennedy's hostility because she was periodically sleeping with him.
Renehan, pp. 134-5. Compounding the sexual intrigue is the fact that (a) Henry was at the same time having an affair with Beaverbrook's grand-daughter, Lady Jean Campbell *(ibid)*, and (b) Clare and Beaverbrook had enjoyed sexual relations: see Ralph G. Martin, *Henry and Clare: An Intimate Portrait of the Luces* (Putnam's, 1991), p. 336.

. . . then go to a radio station, where, on a nationwide hook-up, he would criticize Roosevelt and endorse Willkie for president.
Renehan, pp. 170-4. Black considers Luce only a peripheral player in this conspiracy, yet many scholars note that Luce was directly involved in the plan —so much so that he even offered to write the speech in which Kennedy would denounce Roosevelt. See Herzstein, p. 153; Koskoff, p. 271; Renehan, p. 135; and John H. Davis, *The Kennedys: Dynasty and Disaster, 1848-1983* (McGraw-Hill, 1984), p. 84.

Page 9

Beaverbrook's secretary would intercept the letters, however, steam them open, copy down the contents, and then pass them on to her cagey employer.
Martin, p. 342.

"My son was shooting down Germans in the air," he explained to Stephenson later. "I was obliged to be ruthless on the ground."
Stevenson, p. 148.

Pages 9–10

I sat back and watched FDR across his cluttered desk. . . . And then, in front of me, he drafted a cable to Kennedy.
Stevenson, p. 149. There is considerable controversy over the accuracy of *The Man Called Intrepid*. Some believe that Stephenson, who suffered a massive stroke in1963, could not distinguish fact from fantasy when he provided information for this book. Two of the sharpest criticisms claim that Stephenson never once spoke with Roosevelt or even knew Beaverbrook. Both charges, however, are untrue. Martin Gilbert documents a conversation between Stephenson and Roosevelt in *Winston S. Churchill, Volume VI: Finest Hour, 1939-1941* (Heinemann, 1983), p. 990. Letters between Stephenson and Beaverbrook can be found in the Beaverbrook Canadian Correspondence, MG H 156, Case 48 (a), File 1c #2, # 29942-29945. UNB Archives, Harriet Irving Library, University of New Brunswick. For more on the *Intrepid* controversy, see Bill Macdonald, *The True Intrepid: Sir William Stephenson and the Unknown Agents* (Dundurn, Sask.: Timberholme Books, 1998), especially chapter 11.

Page 10

Kennedy followed these instructions, saying little to the throng of reporters who greeted him in New York and pressured him on his rumoured defection to the Willkie camp.
Beschloss, p. 17. See also Smith, p. 475.

"Ah, Joe, old friend," Roosevelt said as he picked up the receiver, "it is so good to hear your voice. Please come to the White House tonight for a little family dinner. I'm dying to talk to you."
Arthur Krock, *Memoirs: Sixty Years on the Firing Line* (Funk & Wagnalls, 1968), p. 399.

It was equally outrageous that the State Department had treated him so "horribly" these past few years, failing to inform him of major military shipments from the United States to Britain.

Ronald Kessler, *The Sins of the Father: Joseph P. Kennedy and the Dynasty He Founded* (Warner Books, 1996), p. 224.

Pages 10–11

"I have never said anything privately in my life that I didn't say to you personally, and I have never said anything in a public interview that ever caused you the slightest embarrassment."

Smith, p. 481.

Page 11

Kennedy, trapped by his own rhetoric, agreed, and Missy LeHand was asked to make arrangements for a spot on national radio.

Kessler, p. 224; Black, p. 591.

"I believe that Franklin D. Roosevelt should be reelected president."

Smith, p. 489.

One was that Beaverbrook maintained an outward loyalty by having his newspapers continue their friendly coverage of Kennedy well after his resignation.

Koskoff, p. 305.

He acutely wanted to be liked, especially by the elites of England.

Ibid., p. 277.

"I have wondered sometimes," wrote his granddaughter Amanda Smith, "whether he didn't share Gladstone's sneaking fondness for a lord. He seems to have been especially susceptible to kind words from peers and royals, noting that the lords Derby or Beaverbrook ('a great admirer of mine, and a terribly smart man') had found his counsel sensible and useful."

Smith, p. xxiii.

He notes with satisfaction that Beaverbrook still mentioned his name often to Roosevelt, and always with "great affection."

Ibid., p. 536

Page 12

"To this end . . . traveled to Europe."
For examples of Joseph Kennedy's warm enjoining of his sons to seek
Beaverbrook's views, see: Joseph P. Kennedy to Robert Kennedy, August 15,
1954 and Joseph P. Kennedy to John F. Kennedy, July 26, 1957, in Smith,
pp. 664-5 & 678.

A meeting with his father's friend was always an honour for John, and
he happily saw Beaverbrook on a trip to Britain in 1945.
Ralph G. Martin, *Seeds of Destruction: Joe Kennedy and His Sons*
(G. P. Putnam's Sons, 1995), p. 134.

Page 13

During the war John had regarded Beaverbrook as a "strong" figure
and even considered him "the logical successor to Churchill."
Nigel Hamilton, *J.F.K.: Reckless Youth* (Random House, 1992), pp. 466-7.

When father Joe learned of the coincidence, he urged his son to spend
time on the voyage with Beaverbrook. Robert reluctantly agreed.
Arthur M. Schlesinger, Jr., *Robert Kennedy and His Times* (Houghton Mifflin
Company, 1978), p. 73.

"He is clever, has good character, energy, a clear understanding,
and fine philosophy. You are sure to hear a great deal of him if you
live long enough."
Ibid., p. 74.

Pages 13–14

"Your papers certainly treated John handsomely."
Smith, p. 688.

Page 14

Relations between father and son did not improve after Teddy finished
military service, for he returned to Harvard only to resume the
carousing he had left behind.
Koskoff, pp. 464-5; Martin, p. 164.

He told him that mistakes made at eighteen did not haunt a man for long, and that many unexpected opportunities still lay ahead of him.
Martin, p. 164.

"Joe said to Ted and me that this good friend of mine has this lovely house in Nassau. And you should go down."
Leamer, Laurence. *The Kennedy Men, 1901-1963: the laws of the father.* (William Morrow, 2001), p. 398.

"It was the worst experience of our life. It was a little cottage, practically a shack, on this tiny island, just sand. We slept on these mats. There were bugs, and it was a nightmare."
Ibid., p. 400.

Page 15

"It has been my purpose for some time," Teddy explained, "to write to you and once again express my great appreciation for your wonderfully warm hospitality which you so graciously extended to Joan and myself on our first and unforgettable visit to Nassau."
Teddy to Beaverbrook, February 15, 1959. Beaverbrook Canadian Correspondence. MG H 156. Case 77, File1(h), #47561-47567. UNB Archives, Harriet Irving Library, University of New Brunswick.

Ted's mother, Rose, wrote to Beaverbrook about the campaign, noting that the Canadian newspapers had done much to bolster Jack's reputation and could likely do the same for Teddy now.
Martin, p. 399.

Ted won the seat easily, becoming at the age of thirty the youngest member in the United States Senate.
Ibid., pp. 399-400.

And so Beaverbrook, deeply involved in the Kennedy family plan, wrote Teddy a letter asking him to take his electoral win in stride and lie low for a while.
Leamer, p. 471.

He was especially fond of one of Beaverbrook's lesser-known books, *Success* (1921), a collection of short biographies about poor boys who made good—boys not unlike Beaverbrook and Kennedy—and set about finding an American publisher for an edition to which he would write an introduction.
Koskoff, pp. 340-41.

The following year, as an additional honour to his friend, Kennedy established the Lord Beaverbrook Chair of Journalism at Notre Dame University.

Kessler, p. 333.

Page 16

"His appointment as chancellor is more than a recognition of his benefactions. . . . . Well might Canadians rank Lord Beaverbrook as their most valuable 'export'."

The Globe and Mail, June 22, 1946, in UNB Archives, Presidents' Papers. UA RG 136, Box 1: A-E (1945-47). File 8: "Beaverbrook". UNB Archives. Harriet Irving Library, University of New Brunswick.

"If Max gets to Heaven he won't last long. He will be chucked out for trying to pull off a merger between Heaven and Hell . . . after having secured a controlling interest in key subsidiary companies in both places, of course."

A. J. P. Taylor, *Beaverbrook* (Simon and Schuster, 1972) p. 164.

Page 17

"He at once set himself up as buyer-in-chief for the university library, though without enquiry into its most pressing needs. The library got what Beaverbrook thought good for it—Calvinist theology, Knox's works, John Galt's *Annals of the Parish*, fine copies of the *Shorter Catechism*."

Ibid., p. 582.

Bailey wrote, "I worked for three years and more with three assistants who did almost nothing else except prepare and process book lists, check the incoming books, and file them away for cataloguing. The books poured in, almost everything we asked for . . . In all there must have been twenty thousand or more."

Alfred Goldsworthy Bailey, *Lord Beaverbrook in New Brunswick: Reminiscences* (unpublished memoir, 1975). Bailey Family Papers, MG H 1, MS. 4.7.1.4, p. 20. UNB Archives, Harriet Irving Library, University of New Brunswick.

Beaverbrook's secretary, Margaret Ince, on whom much of the burden of coordinating the search fell, estimated that she had used 236 booksellers throughout England, Scotland and Wales, plus another 161 in London, not counting publishing houses.

Memo (#23) from Margaret Ince to Beaverbrook. Beaverbrook Canadian Correspondence. MG H 156, Case 8a, File 5a, # 4096. UNB Archives. Harriet Irving Library, University of New Brunswick.

"I venture to advise you never to buy a book written about a man by his wife. There is no such thing as a good book by a wife about her husband unless you except the book about Arnold Bennett by his wife —and then only because his wife hated him."

Letter from Beaverbrook to Bailey, 16 December 1950. Beaverbrook Canadian Correspondence. MG H 156, Case 8a, File 5a, #4003. UNB Archives. Harriet Irving Library, University of New Brunswick.

Of the Kinsey *Report on Sexual Behavior in the Human Male*, he advised: "You will have to consider whether you are going to put this book into the general Library or place it under control. It seems to me that, in any case, when the new Library Wing is opened, it would be better to hide it in some obscure place. And after a little time, produce it."

Letter from Beaverbrook to Bailey, 11 December 1950, Beaverbrook Canadian Correspondence. MG H 156, Case 8a, File 5a, #4006. UNB Archives. Harriet Irving Library. University of New Brunswick.

He also provided some rare, if eclectic manuscripts, including several purported to have been written by Louis Riel, and letters by William Pitt the Younger, Thomas Jefferson, and Lord Nelson. Inevitably, the item that generated greatest public interest was "Lord Nelson's letter to Lady Hamilton in which," as Lord Beaverbrook insisted, "he accused her of infidelity."

Bailey Family Papers, MG H 1, MS 4.7.1.4, pp. 21-2. UNB Archives. Harriet Irving Library. University of New Brunswick. Letter from Nelson to Lady Hamilton, dated 9 March 1801; written from Yarmouth, England when Nelson was preparing, along with the commander, Sir Hyde Parker, to engage the Danes in the Battle of Copenhagen. The letter is in the Beaverbrook Collection of Manuscripts, [BC-MS # 154], UNB Archives. Harriet Irving Library. University of New Brunswick.

A sample list of donors to the Beaverbrook collection, 1951 and earlier, bears eloquent witness to Beaverbrook's circle of acquaintance: Winston Churchill, Franklin Delano Roosevelt, the Marquess of Queensbury, Lady Lloyd George, William Randolf Hearst, the Right Honourable Richard Law, the Smithsonian Institution, the Metropolitan Museum of Art, and the Carnegie Corporation.

Some of the letters are in the Beaverbrook Collection of Manuscripts [BC-MS], UNB Archives. Harriet Irving Library. University of New Brunswick. Some are in the Beaverbrook Canadian Correspondence, MG H 156 in the UNB Archives.

Page 18

"He required me to give him a list of the books that he
wanted for the open shelves of his new and lovely room...."
Albert W. Trueman, *A Second View of Things: A Memoir* (McClelland and
Stewart, 1982), p. 104.

Page 19

The Latin motto, taken from Psalm 38:21, emblazoned above the
Bonar Law-Bennett Library entrance was *Ne me derelinquas, Domine*
(forsake me not, O Lord). A more popular local translation, however,
at least among those who feared that Beaverbrook's great generosity
might one day come to an abrupt end, was "Forsake us not, your
Lordship."
Ibid., p. 99.

A more public and dramatic example of Beaverbrook's tendency to
exercise unassigned authority occurred in 1953 when Dr. Trueman,
resigned, partly out of frustration with the chancellor.
See Bailey, pp.25-6.; and Trueman, Ch. 13.

Page 20

On returning home, the Premier informed the nominating committee
of the University of New Brunswick's governing body that Lord
Beaverbrook had made a choice, which prompted the members to
resign in protest.
Bailey, pp. 27-8.

"Well, it's unanimous. None of them want you."
Susan Montague, *A Pictorial History of the University of New Brunswick*
(University of New Brunswick, 1992), p. 96.

The provincial government pleaded with him to reconsider. . . .
Before long the government decided to introduce a bill in the
legislature to reappoint him under the slightly different title of
"Honorary Life Chancellor."
Bailey, p. 28.

"I hope the boy Mackay will stand up to his responsibilities. ..."
Letter from Beaverbrook to Mary Louise Lynch, 9 September 1953. MG
H148, file 1952-1954. UNB Archives. Harriet Irving Library, University of New
Brunswick. {Note: The Mary Louise Lynch correspondence is closed until
2012. I am privy to the correspondence by permission of Miss Lynch.}

Page 21

Beaverbrook "imagined that he could appoint a university president,
just as he appointed a newspaper editor, and the event showed that he
could. Mackay proved to be an energetic president, devoted to
Beaverbrook's interests."
Taylor, p. 611.

Page 22

Between June 1947 and July 1948 there was a steady drizzle of
correspondence among the Maritime Stock Breeders Association, the
Canadian Ayreshire Breeders Association, the New Brunswick Minister
of Agriculture, A. C. Taylor, and Beaverbrook.
Beaverbrook Canadian Correspondence, MG H156. Case 1a, file 3,
#113-189. UNB Archives, Harriet Irving Library, University of New Brunswick.

Taylor confirms Beaverbrook's preference to see the bull "enjoy his
labours," having been advised, "it is not your wish to have the bull used
artificially . . . but rather that he is to be used in the top Ayreshire herds
in the normal breeding manner."
Beaverbrook Canadian Correspondence, MG H156. Case 1a, file 3, # 117
(25 July 1947). Letter from Austin C. Taylor, Minister of Agriculture, to
Beaverbrook. Archives & Special Collections, Harriet Irving Library,
University of New Brunswick.

Page 23

"Lord Beaverbrook has conferred many benefits on New Brunswick,"
Muggeridge acknowledged, "but not by stealth…"
Malcolm Muggeridge, "The cult the Beaver built." *Maclean's Magazine*
(November 2, 1963), pp. 20-21, 60-2, 64.

Presidents Trueman, Mackay, and Professor Bailey, though frequently
inconvenienced, sometimes browbeaten, and occasionally hurt by
Beaverbrook's caprice, all shared the view that he was crucial to the
development of their university.
See, for example, Trueman, pp. 108-09, and Bailey, p. 29 and *passim*.

Page 24

According to Colin Mackay, Beaverbrook had felt that there were
gaps in his education and knowledge, especially in the fields of literature
and the arts.
Taped interview with Colin B. Mackay, December, 1990, in possession of
James Downey.

"He was a rampaging individualist . . . and he always favoured the
rambustious, marauding private enterprise system."
Foot, p. 81

"But in peace, as in war, do not tread too long the way which
paralyzes individualism or the power to act will be atrophied...
There is no substitute for the individual."
UA Case 67, Box 1. UNB Archives.

Pages 24-5

"I give you my own beliefs. . . . These two functions of the university
must never be lost sight of. In my opinion, they excel in importance even
the task of providing educated and competent young people to fill posts
of responsibility in industry and the professions."
Speech given at the inauguration of John Bassett as Chancellor of Bishop's
University, in Lennoxville, Quebec, 26 October 1950. Beaverbrook Canadian
Correspondence. MG H 156. C52(a), File 21 #32119-32120. UNB Archives.

Page 26

. . . a few others, including Salvador Dali and Nikita Khrushchev,
reluctantly declined.
See exchange of letters between Beaverbrook and Dali, July 1959, in
Beaverbrook Papers, C28F1c #16490 and #16492 MG H 156, Case 28, File
1c, #16490 -16492. Archives & Special Collections, Harriet Irving Library,
University of New Brunswick. Khrushchev was ready to accept Beaverbrook's
invitation to the 1960 convocation until Prime Minister John Diefenbaker
made a speech at the United Nations denouncing the Soviet Leader. See
letter from Anne Eaton to Beaverbrook, October 6, 1960, Beaverbrook
Canadian Correspondence, MG H 156. Case 91, File 5, # 55688.

Page 27

The day before, he wrote to a friend that Fredericton "is lively again with the arrival of Senator Kennedy and the multitude that has come to see him."

Beaverbrook to Nell Martin, October 7, 1957, Beaverbrook Canadian Correspondence, MG H 156. Case 136, File 9, # 83225, UNB Archives.

"When he has become President of the United States of America, I say to him, remember New Brunswick. Full development of the Beechwood Power Project on the St. John River depends largely on water storage in the State of Maine. Remember us in the days when you are become President and give us a great dam in the State of Maine."

Fredericton *Daily Gleaner* (October 8, 1957), p. 1.
For an account of this event, see Ted Jones, "Remembering the Kennedys," in *The Atlantic Advocate,* October 1982, pp. 12-18.

Page 28

The most recent stays, which were also some of the longest, forced him to cancel many speaking engagements or have Robert, among others, appear on his behalf.

Robert Dallek, "The Medical Ordeals of JFK," *Atlantic Monthly* (December, 2002), p. 58; Leamer, p. 379.

That he made it to New Brunswick for the October 8 convocation was little short of miraculous, and Beaverbrook, would have known that his friend Joe Kennedy had prevailed upon his son to come.

Writing to Colin Mackay, on August 29, 1957, Beaverbrook acknowledged, "We do not owe Senator Kennedy's presence to me, but to his father, Joseph P. Kennedy, my very close friend and near neighbour on the Riviera." Beaverbrook Canadian Correspondence, MG H 156. Case 111 (a), File 4, #65543. UNB Archives.

In presenting Kennedy, the University Orator, Robert E.D. Cattley, in the tradition of academic address, paid florid tribute to the honouree. . .

Cattley, Robert E.D. *Honoris causa. The effervescences of a university orator.* [Fredericton]: The Associated Alumnae of the University of New Brunswick, 1968.

Convocation, October 1957. John Fitzgerald Kennedy to be Doctor of Laws, pp. 62-3. See also: http://www.lib.unb.ca/archives/HonoraryDegrees/ for text of citation and convocation address.

Page 29

Kennedy's "Good Fences Make Good Neighbours" speech, likely co-authored by Theodore Sorensen . . .

From: Theodore C Sorensen <tsorensen@paulweiss.com>
To: James Downey <jdowney@admmail.uwaterloo.ca>
Date: Wed, 25 Aug 2004 16:45:55 -0400
Subject: UNB Speech
It was a long time ago, but I believe that the University of New Brunswick speech was one of those on which I helped then Senator Kennedy. But I have no recollection of the drafting process for that particular talk or of any comments made by JFK with respect to Lord Beaverbrook. I would only note the fact that a great deal of care and thought was put into a well-crafted speech—which could be said of every JFK speech. He took every speech and audience seriously and insisted on being well prepared.

Page 30

"It is treated, nowadays, with all the respect which is accorded automatically to an important and...above all...to a significant document. Washington correspondents of Canadian newspapers wouldn't be caught without it. The various departments of the Canadian Government have examined it, scrutinized it and dissected it. Experts in Canadian-American relations have gone over it with a fine-tooth comb in search of passages which might be expected to have special meaning for our time."

Arthur Blakely, "The Man from Massachusetts," *Montreal Gazette*, April 10, 1961. Presidents' Papers, UA RG 136, Box 43, file 43 (1961-1963). UNB Archives.

"He's a hothead. He's a fool—too young, too brash, too inexperienced, and a boastful son of a bitch!"

Knowlton Nash, *Kennedy and Diefenbaker: Fear and Loathing across the Undefended Border* (McClelland & Stewart, 1990), p. 11.

Page 31

Meanwhile Kennedy told friends that Diefenbaker was a "grandstanding, insincere, sanctimonious, platitudinous old bore."
Ibid, p. 12.

Robert Kennedy would say, years later, "My brother really hated John Diefenbaker. He thought him a contemptible old fool. In fact, you know, my brother really hated only two men in all his presidency. One was Sukarno [dictator of Indonesia] and the other was Diefenbaker."

Ibid, p 11.

"[The] repercussions of their animosity spread across the whole canvas of politics, officialdom, and bureaucracy. In some cases, normal Canada-U.S. relations simply collapsed."

Ibid, see especially ch. 4. See also J. L. Granatstein, "When Push Came to Shove: Canada and the United States," in *Kennedy's Quest for Victory: American Foreign Policy, 1961-1963,* ed. Thomas G. Paterson (Oxford University Press, 1989), pp. 86-104.

When Diefenbaker's conservative government was defeated by Lester Pearson's liberals in the spring of 1963, he blamed defeat on Washington, describing it as a Kennedy-engineered *coup d'état*.

Nash, p. 14.

"The great artist is thus a solitary figure. He has, as Frost said, a lover's quarrel with the world. In pursuing his perceptions of reality, he must often sail against the currents of his time. This is not a popular role. If Robert Frost was much honored in his lifetime, it was because a good many preferred to ignore his darker truths."

President John F. Kennedy Pays Tribute to the Poet Robert Frost and All of America's Writers and Artists, in *In Our Own Words: Extraordinary Speeches of the American Century,* edited by Robert Toricelli and Andrew Carroll (Kodansha International, 1999). p.243.

Page 35

"Looking back now on your own career, I am convinced that had you not had to strive so hard in your early years for money...you would have had a term or two in the White House yourself."

Beschloss, p. 272.

Page 36

"May Joe find solace," Beaverbrook wrote to Rose, "in the assurance that Robert will repeat John's career."

Leamer, p. 741.

"The effect of Kennedy's death is, of course, bad — but not so bad as many newspapers report."

Beaverbrook to John G. McConnell (of the Montreal Star), November 26, 1963. Beaverbrook Canadian Correspondence, MG H 156. Case 106, File 1c (1), # 62918. UNB Archives.

Beaverbrook made no public objection to the site, but said privately that he would donate money towards the plaque only if it were placed somewhere else.

Beaverbrook to J.M.S. Wardell, January 17, 1964. Beaverbrook Canadian Correspondence, MG H156. Case 134, File 1(b), #82058. UNB Archives.

He was too old and feeble, however, to make a fuss, and he died before the unveiling of the memorial in 1965.

The Kennedy memorial plaque was removed from its downtown location, across from the Beaverbrook statute, in 1990, and placed in the Alumni Memorial Building on the UNB campus in 1994.

Page 37

He imbued his sons with his own competitive spirit, and never failed to be engaged with their lives and careers.

Martin, *Seeds of Destruction,* p. xviii and *passim.*

He set up income trusts for his children so that they might choose careers of public service if they so wished.

"Man Out Front", *Time Magazine,* December 2, 1957.

"What it really adds up to is love . . . We therefore have a responsibility to others who are less well off."

Quoted by Edward Kennedy in his eulogy to his brother, Robert. See *In Our Own Words.* Toricelli and Carroll, p. 274.

Page 39

Beaverbrook became a more indulgent and supportive grandfather than he ever was a father.

Chisholm and Davie, p. 518.

"I loved him, not merely as a friend but as a second father, even though throughout I had . . . the most excellent of fathers of my own."

Foot, p. 79.

"I loved Max Aitken Lord Beaverbrook when he was alive. Now that I have learnt to know him better from his records I love him even more."

Taylor, p. xvii. It seems, however, that Taylor would have something of a change of heart later. In 1976 he wrote: "Ten years ago I was looking forward to writing Beaverbrook's life and I enjoyed writing it. Now in retrospect it seems a waste of time: he was not really worth a book on that scale." Kathleen Burk, *Troublemaker: The Life and History of A. J. P. Taylor* (Yale university Press, 2000), p 324.

Page 40

At convocation he was introduced by the same University Orator, Professor Robert E. D. Cattley.

Cattley, Robert E.D. *Honoris causa. The effervescences of a university orator.* [Fredericton]: The Associated Alumnae of the University of New Brunswick, 1968. Convocation, October 1967. "Robert Francis Kennedy to be Doctor of Laws," pp. 146-7.

Page 41

It was "Vive New Brunswick Libre."

See the typescript of the speech in the UNB Archives. UA Case 69, Box 1.

Page 43

RFK employs a few lyrical phrases he used the previous year in a speech to young South Africans in his Day of Affirmation address at Cape Town University of: Youth "is not a time of life, but a state of mind; a temper of the will; a quality of the imagination; a predominance of courage over timidity, of the appetite for adventure over the love of ease."

A Patriot's Handbook: songs, poems, stories, and speeches celebrating the land we love, selected and introduced by Caroline Kennedy, Hyperion, NY, 2003, p.381

Page 44

"Come down and vote in the United States sometime."

Ted Jones, in *The Atlantic Advocate,* October, 1982, p. 18

"I find Bobby a most lively character with an exceedingly aggressive mind, well-balanced, clear in statement, powerful in argument, well-read and bound to do a great deal in life."

Beaverbrook Papers. House of Lords Library, London, UK. Dec. 11, 1957. Quoted in Martin, *Seeds of Destruction*, p. 487.

The passage he used for his UNB address was one that he had copied himself into his daybook.

Evan Thomas, *Robert Kennedy: His Life* (Simon & Schuster, 2000), pp. 319-20.

Pages 44-5

From remarks by Senator Robert F. Kennedy on the death of the Reverend Martin Luther King, at a rally in Indianapolis, Indiana, April 4, 1968, as quoted in

Arthur M. Schlesinger, Jr., *Robert Kennedy and His Times* (Boston: Houghton Mifflin Company, 1978), 875, 1020 n.84."

Page 45

"Those guys who can make the rafters ring with hokum—well, I guess that's O.K., but it keeps me from being an effective political speaker."

"Man Out Front," in *Time Magazine*, December 2, 1957.

Page 47

Early in his career he had considered himself a mediocre speaker...

Dallek, *An Unfinished Life: John F. Kennedy 1917-1963*, (Little, Brown & Co, 2003, New York), pp. 124-5.

Page 48

In 1957 he had received more than 2500 speaking invitations, and had accepted 144.

"Man Out Front," *Time Magazine*, December 2, 1957.

Canada has had its fair share of gifted talkers (none better than Beaverbrook himself) . . . "Arnold Bennett, no mean talker surely, called [Beaverbrook] the best dramatic raconteur he ever heard."

Foot, p. 84.

✿✿✿✿✿

Lord Beaverbrook
and the Kennedys

Bibliography:
Books, Articles, Manuscripts

BOOKS:

Beaverbrook, Max Aitken, Baron   *My early life.* Fredericton: Brunswick Press, 1965

Beaverbrook, Max Aitken, Baron   *Success.* McClelland & Stewart, 1921

Beschloss, Michael R.   *Kennedy and Roosevelt: the uneasy alliance.* W.W. Norton, 1980

Black, Conrad   *Franklin Delano Roosevelt: champion of freedom.* Public Affairs, 2003

Burk, Kathleen   *Troublemaker: the life and history of A.J. P. Taylor.* Yale UP, 2000

Carlisle, Rodney P.   *Hearst and the new deal: the progressive as reactionary.* Garland Publishing, 1979

Cattley, Robert E. D.   *Honoris causa. The effervescences of a university orator.* Fredericton: The Associated Alumnae for the University of New Brunswick, 1968

Chester, Lewis and Jonathan Fenby   *The fall of the house of Beaverbrook.* Andre Deutsch, 1979

Chisholm, Anne and Michael Davie   *Beaverbrook: a life.* Hutchinson, 1992

Dallek, Robert   *An unfinished life: John F. Kennedy 1917-1963.* Little, Brown & Co, 2003

Davis, John H.   *The Kennedys: dynasty and disaster, 1848-1983.* McGraw-Hill, 1984

Foot, Michael   *Debts of honour.* Davis Poynter Ltd., 1980

Gilbert, Martin   *Winston S. Churchill. Volume VI: Finest hour, 1939-1941.* Heinemann, 1983

Goldwin, Robert A. and Harry M. Clor, eds.   *Readings in American foreign policy,* 2nd ed., OUP 1971

Goodwin, Doris Kearns   *No ordinary time: Franklin and Eleanor Roosevelt; The home front in world war II.* Simon and Schuster, 1994

Greunding, Dennis, ed.   *Great Canadian speeches.* Fitzhenry & Whiteside, 2004

Hamilton, Nigel   *J.F.K.: reckless youth.* Random House, 1992

Harriman, Averell W. and Elie Abel   *Special Envoy to Churchill and Stalin, 1941-1946.* Random House, 1976

Harvey, John, ed.   *The diplomatic diaries of Oliver Harvey, 1937-1940.* Clear-Type Press, 1970

Herzstein, Robert E.   *Henry R. Luce: a political portrait of the man who created the American century.* Scribner's 1994

Kessler, Ronald   *The sins of the father: Joseph P. Kennedy and the dynasty he founded.* Warner Books, 1996

Kinsella, William R., Jr.   *Leadership in Isolation: FDR and the origins of the second world war.* Schenkman Publishing, 1978

Koskoff, David E.   *Joseph P. Kennedy: a life and times.* Prentice-Hall, 1974

Krock, Arthur   *Memoirs: sixty years on the firing line.* Funk & Wagnalls, 1968

Leamer, Laurence   *The Kennedy Men, 1901-1963: The Laws of the Father.* William Morrow, 2001

Lysaght, Charles   *Brendan Bracken.* Allen Lane, 1979

Macdonald, Bill   *The true intrepid: Sir William Stephenson and the unknown agents.* Timberholme Books, 1998

Marchildon, Gregory P.

Profits and politics: Beaverbrook and the gilded age of Canadian finance. University of Toronto Press, 1996

Martin, Ralph G.

Henry and Clare: an intimate portrait of the Luces. Putnam's, 1991

Martin, Ralph G.

Seeds of destruction: Joe Kennedy and his sons. G. P. Putnam's Sons, 1995

Montague, Susan

A pictorial history of the University of New Brunswick. Fredericton: UNB, 1992

Nash, Knowlton

Kennedy and Diefenbaker: fear and loathing across the undefended border. McClelland & Stewart, 1990

Paterson, Thomas G., ed.

Kennedy's quest for victory: American foreign policy, 1961-1963. OUP, 1989

Renehan, Edward J.

The Kennedys at war. Doubleday, 2002

Schlesinger, Arthur M., Jr.

Robert Kennedy and his times. Houghton Mifflin Co., 1978

Smith, Amanda, ed.

Hostage to fortune: the letters of Joseph P. Kennedy. Viking, 2001

Stevenson, William

A man called intrepid: the secret war. Harcourt Brace Jovanovich, 1976

Swanberg, W. A.

Citizen Hearst: a biography of William Randolph Hearst. Scribner's, 1961

Taylor, A. J. P.

Beaverbrook. Simon and Schuster, 1972

Thomas, Evan

Robert Kennedy: his life. Simon and Schuster, 2000.

Torricelli, Robert and Andrew Carroll, eds

In our own words. Kodansha International, 1999

Trueman, Albert W.

A second view of things: a memoir. McClelland & Stewart, 1982

ARTICLES:

Blakely, Arthur	*The Man from Massachusetts.* Montreal Gazette (10 April 1961). Column heading is "Ottawa… day by day".
Dallek, Robert	"The medical ordeals of JFK." *Atlantic Monthly* (December 2002): Vol. 290, Iss. 5; pg. 49, (1 pg) cover story
Jones, Ted	"Remembering the Kennedys." *The Atlantic Advocate* (October 1982): 12-18
Muggeridge, Malcolm	"The cult the Beaver built." *Maclean's Magazine* (2 November 1963): 20-21; 60-62, 64
n.a.	"U.S. Senator, Canadian cabinet minister are honoured by UNB." *Daily Gleaner* (8 October 1957): 1
n.a.	"Democrats: Man out front." *Time Magazine* (2 December 1957) [vol. LXX, no. 23; cover story; no author or pagination online]

http://www.time.com/time/magazine/0,9263,7601571202,00.html

❀❀❀❀❀

MANUSCRIPTS:

Bailey, Alfred G.   "Lord Beaverbrook in New Brunswick.
                                     Reminiscences." UNB. Bailey Family Papers.
                                     MG H 1. See MS 4.7.1.3 (62p.)

UNB. BC-MS

UNB. Beaverbrook Canadian Correspondence. MG H 156

UNB. Presidents' Papers. UA RG 136

UNB. Mary Louise Lynch Correspondence. MG H 148/149

UNB. UA Cases

❀❀❀❀❀

Photo: Scot Filler

James Downey
is a graduate of Memorial
University of Newfoundland and the
University of London.
He taught English literature
at Carleton University before falling
from grace into academic administration.
He has been president
of Carleton University, the University
of New Brunswick, and the University
of Waterloo where he is now
President Emeritus.